COMPREHENSION: GRADE 5
TABLE OF CONTENTS

D0815254

© Steck-Vaughn Company

COMPREHENSION: GRADE 5

INTRODUCTION

This book is designed to help students become better readers. The IRA/NCTE Standards for the English Language Arts lists as their first recommendation: "Students read a wide range of print and nonprint texts to build an understanding of texts, of themselves, and of the cultures of the United States and the world; to acquire new information; to respond to the needs and demands of society and the workplace; and for personal fulfillment. Among these texts are fiction and nonfiction, classic and contemporary works." A variety of reading selections attract and hold the interest of students. The activities in this book contain high-interest reading selections that cover a wide range of subjects in such areas as science, social studies, history, sports, and the arts.

ORGANIZATION

Each of the six units focuses on essential reading comprehension skills: finding the facts, detecting a sequence, learning new vocabulary through context, identifying the main idea, drawing conclusions, and making inferences.

- **FACTS:** Literal comprehension is a foundation skill for understanding a reading selection. Students using the Facts unit practice identifying pieces of factual information presented in each reading selection. The focus is on specific details that tell *who, what, when, where,* and *how.*
- **SEQUENCE:** Sequence involves the time order of events and the temporal relationship of one event or step to other events or steps. Reading for sequence means identifying the order of events in a story or the steps in a process.
- **CONTEXT:** When students practice using context, they must use all the words in a reading selection to understand the unfamiliar words. As they develop this skill, students become aware of the relationships between words, phrases, and sentences. The skill provides them with a tool that helps them understand words and concepts by learning how language is used to express meaning. Mastering this skill allows students to become independent readers.
- **MAIN IDEA:** When students read for the main idea, they must read to recognize the overall point made in the reading selection. Students must be able to differentiate the details from the main idea. They must understand the one idea that is supported by all the details in the selection. Identifying the main idea involves recognizing or making a generalization about a group of specifics.
- **CONCLUSION:** Drawing a conclusion is a complex reading skill because a conclusion is not stated in a reading selection. Students are asked to draw a conclusion based only on the information within a selection. They must put together the details from the information as if they were clues to a puzzle. The conclusion they draw must be supported by the details in the reading selection.
- **INFERENCE:** Students make inferences by combining their own knowledge and experiences with what they read. They must consider all the facts in the reading selection. Then they must put together those facts and what they already know to make a reasonable inference about something that is not stated in the selection. Making an inference requires students to go beyond the information in the text.

© Steck-Vaughn Company

USE

The activities in this book are designed for independent use by students who have had instruction in the specific skills covered in the lessons. Copies of the activity sheets can be given to individuals or pairs of students for completion. When students are familiar with the content of the worksheets, they can be assigned as homework.

To begin, determine the implementation that fits your students' needs and your classroom structure. The following plan suggests a format for this implementation.

1. **Administer** the Assessment Test to establish baseline information on each student. This test may also be used as a post-test when the student has completed a unit.
2. **Explain** the purpose of the worksheets to the class.
3. **Review** the mechanics of how you want students to work with the activities. Do you want them to work in pairs? Are the activities for homework?
4. **Introduce** students to the process and purpose of the activities. Work with students when they have difficulty. Give them only a few pages at a time to avoid pressure.
5. **Do** a practice activity together. Review with students how to do each comprehension skill.

OVERVIEW: FACTS

Introducing the Skill

Remind students that facts are things you can taste, touch, feel, smell, and see. Explain that successful readers pay close attention to details. Emphasize that the questions in the Facts unit ask about details stated in the reading selections. Students should be able to show where the answer to a question is located in a selection.

How the Lessons Are Organized

A lesson consists of a reading selection about a single topic broken into two parts. Each part is followed by five questions that require students to find restated facts from the selection.

Practice Activity

Read this story to your students.

The *Titanic*

On April 10, 1912, the *Titanic* left England on its first trip. It was the largest and one of the safest ships ever built. Many rich and famous people were on board. They planned to arrive in New York in six days. But on the night of April 14, the ship ran into an iceberg. The iceberg tore a huge hole in the ship's side. The passengers climbed into lifeboats as the ship began to sink. But there were not enough boats for everyone. Only 711 of the 2,207 people on board lived to tell about the shipwreck.

Have students answer the following questions about the story.

1. How many people lived to tell about the shipwreck?

A. 2,207	C. 500
<u>B. 711</u>	D. 947

2. The *Titanic* was sailing to

A. England	<u>C. New York</u>
B. Paris	D. Iceland

3. When did the *Titanic* leave England?

<u>A. April 10, 1912</u>	C. June 4, 1912
B. March 1, 1912	D. April 14, 1912

Explain to students that they should look for facts while reading the stories. They should read each question carefully and try to find a sentence in the story that has some of the same words as the question.

OVERVIEW: SEQUENCE

Introducing the Skill

Remind students that when they read, the events or steps presented in a story have a special sequence. Explain that clue words, like *today, then, first, after, then,* and *finally,* can help them find what happens first, next, and last in a story. Tell students that sequence can also be implied. Finding sequence without signal words means paying careful attention to verb tense. Another clue to implied sequence is the order in which information is presented. Students need to know that writers usually try to relate the events in a story in order. If there are no time signals, students can assume that events have occurred in the order in which they are presented.

How the Lessons Are Organized

A lesson consists of a reading selection about a single topic, followed by five questions. The first question asks students to put statements in order based on the information in each selection. The following questions ask about the stated or implied sequence in each selection.

Practice Activity

Read this story to your students.

Many people try to protect nature now. But one hundred years ago, few people thought about it. John Muir helped change that. Muir was born in Scotland. Later he moved with his family to a farm in Wisconsin. He loved nature. He also loved to invent things. But in 1867 an accident almost cost him an eye. Muir gave up inventing. That same year he began a thousand-mile walk to the Gulf of Mexico. Later he wrote a book about the plants and animals he saw. In 1868 he went to the Yosemite Valley in California. He spent six years exploring this part of the West. Muir became convinced that the government needed to save areas of great beauty. In 1890 Muir persuaded Congress to set up Yosemite and Sequoia National Parks. In 1892 he founded the Sierra Club.

Have students answer the following questions about the story.

1. Put these events in the order that they happened. What happened first, second, last?
   Muir explored the Yosemite Valley. (2)
   Muir moved to Wisconsin. (1)
   Congress set up two national parks. (3)

2. When was the Sierra Club founded?
   A. before Muir went on the thousand-mile walk
   <u>B. after Yosemite became a national park</u>
   C. while Muir was an inventor

3. What happened just before Muir walked to the Gulf of Mexico?
   A. he wrote a book about what he saw
   B. he grew up on a farm
   <u>C. he almost lost an eye</u>

Explain to students that they should find words in the questions that are the same as words in the story, find time words in the story, and look at the order of the events in the story.

OVERVIEW: CONTEXT

Introducing the Skill

Review this skill with students by using a simple cloze-type procedure. Ask students to supply the missing word in "The pretty, yellow ___ swam happily in the pond." Discuss how they know the word is *fish.* Remind students to pay attention to the meaning of surrounding words and phrases. Also, have them focus on language clues such as the position of the unknown or missing word in the sentence and what kind of words come before and after it.

How the Lessons Are Organized

A lesson consists of four reading selections. In lessons 1 through 6, the selections are presented in a cloze format with two missing words in each selection. In lessons 7 through 12, the selections contain a word in boldface type. Students are asked to use the context of the selection to choose the correct definition for each boldfaced word.

Practice Activity

Read this story to your students.

Elizabeth Blackwell was the first woman doctor in the United States. She tried to get into many <u>(1)</u> schools before she was finally accepted. Later she opened a hospital. It was run <u>(2)</u> by women.

1. A. music B. <u>medical</u> C. beauty D. special
2. A. <u>entirely</u> B. darkly C. softly D. fast

Daffodils are a sign that spring has arrived. Their bright yellow color and long, thin leaves are easy to spot. Wild daffodils cover entire hillsides in the country. Other kinds are found in city yards and parks.

3. In this paragraph, the word **daffodils** means

A. a kind of bird C. a kind of animal
B. <u>a kind of flower</u> D. a kind of kite

Remind students that to use context, they should keep reading even if they find a word they do not know. The right answer is the word that goes with the other words in the story. If they can't find the answer the first time, tell them to look back at the story.

OVERVIEW: MAIN IDEA

Introducing the Skill
Have students recall a movie that they have recently seen. Ask them to state the plot of the movie, using one sentence. Explain that this sentence is the main idea of the movie. Point out the difference between the main idea of the movie and the details that support the main idea. Stress that all of the details add up to the main idea.

How the Lessons Are Organized
A lesson consists of three short reading selections for which students are asked to identify the main idea. Lessons 1 through 6 have stated main ideas, while units 7 through 12 have implied main ideas.

Practice Activity
Read this story to your students.

> You've heard of a full moon and a new moon, but have you heard of a blue moon? Once in a while, there are two full moons in one month. We call the second moon a blue moon. A blue moon appears about every 32 months. So if something happens once in a blue moon, it doesn't happen often.

The story mainly tells

A. why the moon looks full

B. how the moon moves

<u>C. what a blue moon is</u>

D. about the different colors of the moon

For Lessons 1 through 6, have students read the whole story. Then ask themselves "Which sentence is the sum of all the other sentences?" Explain that that will be the main idea.

For Lessons 7 through 12, have students read the whole story. Then they should figure out what the details have in common. Tell them to think about what the writer is trying to tell them.

OVERVIEW: CONCLUSION

Introducing the Skill

Emphasize that practicing this skill means thinking about what is actually stated in the reading selection. Ask students what they can conclude from the sentence, "Sylvia rushed into the kitchen and yanked the cookies from the smoking oven." Students can conclude that Sylvia was not in the kitchen before she pulled the cookies out of the oven. Point out that the sentence states that "Sylvia rushed into the kitchen." Students cannot conclude that Sylvia was baking the cookies, although they could infer this, because the sentence gives no evidence to support that conclusion. Perhaps another family member or friend was baking the cookies. Remind students that the conclusion they draw must be supported by the information in the selection in order to be a correct, or logical, conclusion.

How the Lessons Are Organized

Each lesson contains three short reading selections for which students are asked to choose a conclusion that can logically be drawn from the information presented. Lessons 7 through 12 are more difficult because students are asked to identify a conclusion that cannot be drawn from the information presented.

Practice Activity

Read this story to your students.

It is four thousand years ago in Egypt. You are standing on the banks of the great Nile River. Nearby you see a large barge carrying cattle. A long, wooden boat with many soldiers is in the middle of the river. It's the king's messenger boat. A little later a boat made of reeds with a big, square sail passes by. It is carrying jars of oil and containers of grain.

From the story you can tell that

A. it is hot in Egypt

<u>B. boats were used to carry different things</u>

C. there were no animals in Egypt

D. the soldiers liked to swim

Remind students to read all the clues in the story. They should find a conclusion that fits all the clues. To make sure that they find the correct conclusion, they should ask, "How do I know this?" They should know because of the clues in the story.

OVERVIEW: INFERENCE

Introducing the Skill

Have students imagine that they are at a friend's house. Tell them there is a cake with candles on one table and many presents on another. Balloons and crepe-paper streamers hang from the ceiling. There are many people there. Ask students to make an inference about why this is a special day for their friend. Discuss what facts and personal knowledge or experiences lead them to infer that their friend is having a birthday party. Remind students that they can make inferences by thinking about what they already know and adding it to the facts given in the reading selection. Point out that facts can be found in the selection but that the inference cannot.

How the Lessons Are Organized

A lesson consists of three short reading selections. Factual and inferential statements follow each reading selection. Students must differentiate the facts in the selection from the inferences that can logically be made.

Practice Activity

Read this story to your students.

> Tim and John played basketball together each day after school. One day Tim started shouting that John was not playing fair. John took his basketball and went home. The next day John didn't show up at the basketball court.

Fact	Inference	
○	○	**A.** Tim and John were friends. (I)
○	○	**B.** Tim and John played basketball together. (F)
○	○	**C.** John took his basketball and went home. (F)
○	○	**D.** John was angry with Tim the next day. (I)

Remind students to keep in mind the difference between facts and inferences. They should think about the facts in the story and what they already know. Encourage them to make an inference by putting together what they know and what they've read.

Dear Parent:

During this school year, our class will be working on a variety of reading skills. We will be completing activity sheets that provide practice in the comprehension skills that can help your child become a better reader. The skills we will be focusing on are: finding the facts, detecting a sequence, learning new vocabulary through context, identifying the main idea, drawing conclusions, and making inferences.

From time to time, I may send home activity sheets. To best help your child, please consider the following suggestions:

- Provide a quiet place to work.
- Go over the directions together.
- Encourage your child to do his or her best.
- Check the lesson when it is complete.
- Go over your child's work, and note improvements as well as problems.

Help your child maintain a positive attitude about reading. Provide as many opportunities for reading with your child as possible. Read books from the library, comics in the newspaper, even cereal boxes. Let your child know that each lesson provides an opportunity to have fun and to learn. Above all, enjoy this time you spend with your child. He or she will feel your support, and skills will improve with each activity completed.

Thank you for your help!

Cordially,

© Steck-Vaughn Company

Name ______________________________ Date ______________

First Signs of Spring

Read the story. Choose the answer that best completes each sentence.

How do you know that spring is on its way? For many Americans the first sign of spring is baseball. In late winter many big league teams head south. They go to training camps in warm states such as Florida and Arizona. There they get ready for the opening of baseball season in early April.

Each team has its own camp. The players spend long days training and getting in shape. They run, hit, throw, and catch. They learn to listen to the coaches and to work together as a team. They also play some practice games against other teams. These are called exhibition games.

Spring training camps are full of hope. New players hope to stay on the team. Other players hope to have their best baseball season. Everyone hopes to be part of a winning team.

_____ **1.** For many people baseball is a sign of

A. season **C.** spring
B. work **D.** winter

_____ **2.** Players go to training camps in Florida and

A. Arizona **C.** April
B. Arkansas **D.** Americans

_____ **3.** The players run, hit, throw, and

A. coach **C.** camp
B. catch **D.** kick

_____ **4.** Practice games are called

A. spring training **C.** spring games
B. winning records **D.** exhibition games

_____ **5.** Spring training camps are full of

A. hope **C.** trees
B. bats **D.** fans

Go on to the next page.

Name ______________________________ Date ______________

What do baseball teams pack when they go south? The list is very long! One team from New York takes 3,600 baseballs, 360 bats, 200 uniforms, and 75 helmets. Baseball teams also take pitching machines. Many teams take trunks full of medicine and bandages.

Each player also packs things for the trip. Some take bicycles, golf clubs, and beach chairs. Others take their own television sets. Players taking their children might pack toys and games.

Large vans move the teams to their training camps. Many helpers load and unload the equipment and baggage. By April it's time to move again. The baseball season has begun.

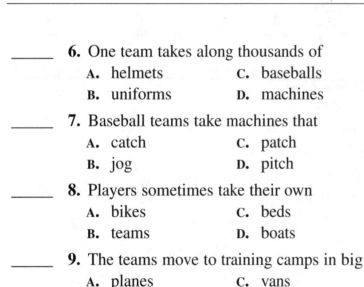

_____ **6.** One team takes along thousands of
- **A.** helmets
- **B.** uniforms
- **C.** baseballs
- **D.** machines

_____ **7.** Baseball teams take machines that
- **A.** catch
- **B.** jog
- **C.** patch
- **D.** pitch

_____ **8.** Players sometimes take their own
- **A.** bikes
- **B.** teams
- **C.** beds
- **D.** boats

_____ **9.** The teams move to training camps in big
- **A.** planes
- **B.** cabs
- **C.** vans
- **D.** workers

_____ **10.** Loading and unloading the trucks takes many
- **A.** days
- **B.** weeks
- **C.** machines
- **D.** helpers

© Steck-Vaughn Company

Name ______________________________ Date ______________

Tale of Tails

Read the story. Choose the answer that best completes each sentence.

Many animals have tails. They use their tails for many different purposes. For instance, some animals use their tails as fly swatters. Have you ever seen a cow flicking its tail back and forth? It's getting rid of bugs. Horses use their tails in this way, too.

Some animals hang by their tails. Monkeys often do this. Then they can use all four of their paws for other things, such as eating. Another animal that uses its tail as a "hanger" is the opossum. The opossum also uses its tail to help it climb trees.

Animals that live in the water use their tails to help them swim. A fish moves its tail from side to side. The rest of its body curves in the opposite direction from its tail. Alligators and crocodiles also swing their tails as they swim. Their large tails give them power and speed.

_____ 1. Animals use their tails for different
- A. periods
- B. purposes
- C. seasons
- D. lengths

_____ 2. An animal that uses its tail as a fly swatter is the
- A. cow
- B. fish
- C. hog
- D. bug

_____ 3. The monkey uses its tail to
- A. swim
- B. climb
- C. hang
- D. talk

_____ 4. A fish moves its tail
- A. up and down
- B. from side to side
- C. in a circle
- D. upside down

_____ 5. Alligators and crocodiles use their tails for
- A. fishing
- B. flying
- C. power
- D. curves

Go on to the next page.

© Steck-Vaughn Company

Name ______________________________ Date ______________

The kangaroo has a large, useful tail. It is like a chair. The kangaroo leans on its tail to rest. The tail is also good for leaping and landing. It helps the kangaroo keep its balance. This is important because an adult kangaroo can leap as far as 15 feet at a time.

A fox has a big, bushy tail. This is a good tail to have on cold nights. The fox can put its tail over its nose and paws while it sleeps. The tail is a blanket that keeps the fox warm.

Some animals don't keep their tails with them at all times. One example is the lizard. If an enemy pulls the lizard's tail in a struggle, the tail breaks off. The lizard leaves its tail and runs to safety. Don't worry! The lizard will soon grow a new tail.

_____ **6.** The kangaroo uses its tail as a place to

- **A.** eat **C.** lean
- **B.** grow **D.** leave

_____ **7.** A kangaroo's tail is also helpful for

- **A.** jumping **C.** walking
- **B.** swimming **D.** crying

_____ **8.** The fox uses its bushy tail as a

- **A.** pillow **C.** chair
- **B.** cover **D.** brush

_____ **9.** A lizard's tail can help the lizard escape from

- **A.** friends **C.** enemies
- **B.** kangaroos **D.** blankets

_____ **10.** The lizard can grow a new

- **A.** fin **C.** nose
- **B.** leg **D.** tail

© Steck-Vaughn Company

Name ______________________________ Date ______________

Cries in the Night

Read the story. Choose the answer that best completes each sentence.

The summer night is quiet. Then suddenly strange, hooting sounds drift through the dark. It seems as if huge owls are flying through the night sky or standing tall on the limbs of trees.

It may be that the hoots are really made by baby birds, or fledglings, that are still in their nest. They are young great horned owls.

Great horned owls have a very long childhood. Most other young birds leave their nests two or three weeks after they hatch. When great horned owls hatch in the early spring, they are blind and helpless. Their parents must take care of them completely for more than two months. When the young owls get hungry at night, they hoot to their parents for food.

_____ **1.** On a summer night, you may hear hoots that seem
- **A.** dark
- **B.** bright
- **C.** quiet
- **D.** strange

_____ **2.** Fledglings are
- **A.** owl nests
- **B.** baby birds
- **C.** adult owls
- **D.** cries for food

_____ **3.** After three weeks, most young birds
- **A.** hatch
- **B.** hoot for food
- **C.** leave their nests
- **D.** are blind

_____ **4.** The young owl's parents must
- **A.** care for them
- **B.** fly away
- **C.** give them lessons
- **D.** make noises

_____ **5.** The little owls hoot when they
- **A.** sit on trees
- **B.** get hungry
- **C.** go to sleep
- **D.** become frightened

Go on to the next page.

© Steck-Vaughn Company

Name ______________________________ Date ______________

The little horned owls grow up to have very keen vision. Unlike some birds, their eyes are set like human eyes. They look directly forward. They see well in all kinds of light. Even in the dim light of a candle, an owl sees things that are a thousand feet away.

An owl has special soft flight feathers all around the edges of its wings. When air brushes through these feathers, there is no sound at all. So, the owl can silently swoop down to catch a mouse or an insect.

When the cool weather of autumn comes, the young owls leave the nest. Their bodies and wings are strong. At last they are ready to live on their own.

_____ **6.** An owl's eyes look
- **A.** sideways
- **B.** dimly
- **C.** ahead
- **D.** warmly

_____ **7.** An owl can see
- **A.** without much light
- **B.** itself
- **C.** vision
- **D.** silently

_____ **8.** The flight feathers help owls
- **A.** move quietly
- **B.** fly quickly
- **C.** grow fast
- **D.** brush air

_____ **9.** Owls like to catch
- **A.** faint sounds
- **B.** mice and bugs
- **C.** rustling leaves
- **D.** big claws

_____ **10.** When fall arrives, young owls are
- **A.** with their parents
- **B.** still learning
- **C.** feeling cold
- **D.** on their own

© Steck-Vaughn Company

Name ______________________________ Date ______________

Simple Ideas

Read the story. Choose the answer that best completes each sentence.

Many objects that people use each day started with a simple idea. These objects have often changed the way we live. Some help us to do a job easier. Others fill a need or solve a problem.

In 1858 H. L. Lipman had such an idea. He took out a pencil, a piece of paper, and an eraser. Then he began to write. Sometimes he needed to change a word. Each time he had to search under his books and papers to find the eraser. "I wish my eraser would stay in one place!" he sighed.

Then Lipman had his simple idea. He cut a groove in one end of the pencil. He glued the eraser into this groove. Lipman had solved his problem. Later he thought that others might like to have such a pencil. So he sold his design. Soon pencils with erasers were common. His design earned him $100,000.

_____ **1.** Useful objects often start with
- **A.** a difficult task
- **B.** a simple idea
- **C.** hard work
- **D.** a committee

_____ **2.** Lipman lost his
- **A.** book
- **B.** paper
- **C.** letter
- **D.** eraser

_____ **3.** Lipman glued his eraser
- **A.** to a pencil
- **B.** inside a book
- **C.** to a pen
- **D.** inside his desk

_____ **4.** Lipman thought his idea would
- **A.** treat an illness
- **B.** help others
- **C.** win a contest
- **D.** cause trouble

_____ **5.** When Lipman sold the design, he
- **A.** made money
- **B.** became famous
- **C.** made new friends
- **D.** took a trip

Go on to the next page.

© Steck-Vaughn Company

Name ______________________________ Date ______________

In 1936 Sylvan N. Goldman solved a problem, too. Goldman owned a grocery store. The people who came into his store had to hold the things they needed in their arms as they shopped. Some people could not carry their groceries easily.

Late one night Goldman worked in his small office. He thought about this problem. Then he had an idea. He pushed two folding chairs together so that the seats were touching. He imagined that there was a large basket on the seats. He imagined that there were wheels on the legs of the chairs. "That's it!" he thought. Then he quickly drew his design for the first grocery cart.

Goldman's first cart was made of wood. Later carts were made of metal. The first metal grocery cart is on display at a museum. The cart is displayed with other objects that make life easier for people. Many of these objects started with a simple idea.

_____ **6.** Sylvan N. Goldman owned a
- **A.** toy store
- **B.** drugstore
- **C.** grocery store
- **D.** bookstore

_____ **7.** The people in Goldman's store had trouble
- **A.** finding things
- **B.** carrying things
- **C.** standing in line
- **D.** paying high prices

_____ **8.** Goldman thought about his problem
- **A.** in his office
- **B.** in a museum
- **C.** on a train
- **D.** at home

_____ **9.** Goldman had his idea when he looked at
- **A.** his small office
- **B.** Lipman
- **C.** erasers
- **D.** two folding chairs

_____ **10.** Goldman's idea made people's lives
- **A.** difficult
- **B.** happier
- **C.** more interesting
- **D.** easier

© Steck-Vaughn Company

Name ______________________ Date ____________

Eating Birds' Nests

Read the story. Choose the answer that best completes each sentence.

Ip hangs three hundred feet above the floor of the dark cave. To reach this place, he climbed a bamboo structure built many years before. He cuts a small object off the wall of the cave. He stuffs it into a burlap bag. There is nothing to protect him from a fall. But Ip does not think of safety. He thinks only of one thing. He wonders how many more swiftlet nests he can gather before the end of the day.

For fifteen hundred years, people like Ip have risked their lives to gather nests of swiftlets. These tiny birds build nests deep inside caves. The caves often have many long and winding tunnels. Some swiftlets fly two miles inside a cave to find a safe place for a nest. Others build nests hundreds of feet above the ground on the ceiling.

_____ **1.** To reach his place in the cave, Ip climbed
- **A.** a wall
- **B.** a ladder
- **C.** ropes
- **D.** a bamboo structure

_____ **2.** Ip uses a burlap bag to
- **A.** protect himself
- **B.** hold his lunch
- **C.** hold nests
- **D.** hold a special tool

_____ **3.** To keep from falling, Ip uses
- **A.** nothing
- **B.** a rope
- **C.** a bamboo structure
- **D.** a burlap bag

_____ **4.** People have gathered swiftlet nests for
- **A.** two years
- **B.** one thousand years
- **C.** three hundred years
- **D.** fifteen hundred years

_____ **5.** Swiftlets build their nests in caves that have
- **A.** wide doors
- **B.** open windows
- **C.** tall trees
- **D.** long tunnels

Go on to the next page.

© Steck-Vaughn Company

Name ______________________________ Date ______________

Swiftlet nests are used to make a soup called bird's nest soup. The dish is made by blending the nests with a rich chicken stock. People in Hong Kong eat a hundred tons of nests each year. There, a bowl of bird's nest soup costs about fifty dollars. Nest gathering provides a good living for Ip.

But Ip does not gather nests just for money. Nest gathering is a tradition. Fathers teach their sons the skills needed for the job. They begin climbing when they are young boys. Many climb after they are grandparents.

Old customs are also passed from father to son. Nest gatherers use a special tool to scrape nests from the caves. It is called a *rada*. No climber would use a different tool. And gatherers place food at the mouths of the caves. They believe that the food and the radas protect them as they climb.

_____ **6.** Swiftlet nests are used to make

- **A.** medicine
- **B.** soup
- **C.** bird cages
- **D.** glue

_____ **7.** One reason Ip gathers nests is

- **A.** to earn money
- **B.** for fun
- **C.** for the thrill
- **D.** to see birds

_____ **8.** Many young boys learn to gather nests from

- **A.** their fathers
- **B.** the swiftlets
- **C.** people in Hong Kong
- **D.** teachers

_____ **9.** A rada is a kind of

- **A.** soup
- **B.** cave
- **C.** bird
- **D.** tool

_____ **10.** Gatherers place food

- **A.** inside nests
- **B.** on the rada
- **C.** at the mouths of caves
- **D.** inside caves

© Steck-Vaughn Company

Name ______________________________ Date ______________

George Washington Carver

Read the story. Choose the answer that best completes each sentence.

The Civil War had ended at last. George, a young freed slave, stood in an apple orchard in Missouri. He was seven years old, and he lived with a German farmer and the farmer's wife. As he breathed the perfume of the trees, the sun warmed his skin. Then he noticed something that worried him. Insects swarmed inside the limbs of one of the trees. He knew the harvest would be ruined if the bugs weren't stopped.

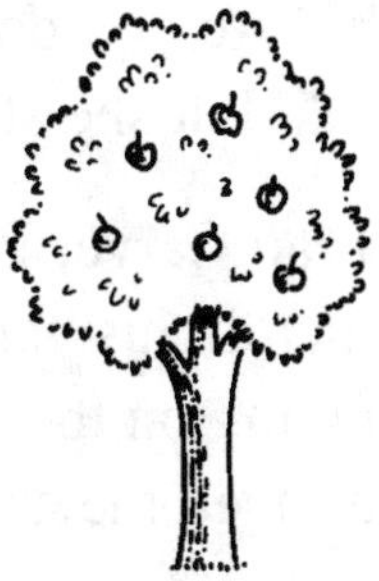

George had a problem. He had never been able to speak clearly. He did not know how he could explain the threat to Farmer Carver. And the farmer would not be able to see the insects because they were inside the tree's limbs. Even though George couldn't speak, he had been born with a special awareness of nature. He knew the bugs were there.

_____ **1.** The story occurs right after

- **A.** World War I **C.** the Civil War
- **B.** World War II **D.** the Revolutionary War

_____ **2.** The apple trees in the story were

- **A.** along a road **C.** in a field
- **B.** near a valley **D.** in an orchard

_____ **3.** George was

- **A.** seven **C.** an old man
- **B.** six **D.** a teenager

_____ **4.** George looked at an apple tree and knew insects were

- **A.** on the leaves **C.** in the apples
- **B.** inside the limbs **D.** in the roots

_____ **5.** When George noticed the insects, he felt

- **A.** happy **C.** worried
- **B.** sad **D.** relaxed

Go on to the next page.

Name ______________________________ Date ______________

George led Farmer Carver to the sick tree. "What do you want? I can't understand you," the farmer said. He went back to work. George sighed. He then tried to tell Frau Carver. Of all the people George knew, she best understood his special language. But she just looked puzzled as he made sounds and pointed at the tree.

George got a saw and began to saw off the bad branches. Farmer Carver raced to him. He shouted angrily, "Stop! What are you doing?" George ran to Frau Carver. He tried to speak, but she still couldn't understand him.

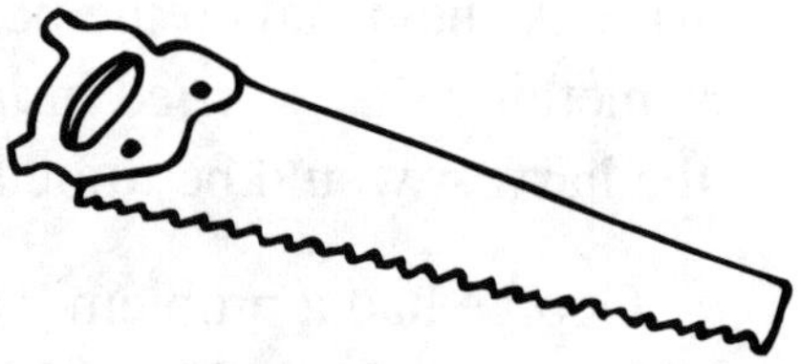

Frau Carver knew George was trying to say something important. She looked at the branch in his hand and gasped. Then she and Farmer Carver both saw the tiny insects crawling on the branch. George, who later was known as Dr. George Washington Carver, had saved the apple harvest.

_____ 6. George's special language was understood by
- A. Farmer Carver
- B. a teacher
- C. a neighbor
- D. Frau Carver

_____ 7. To cut the branches off the tree, George used
- A. a saw
- B. an ax
- C. a hatchet
- D. a knife

_____ 8. The farmer saw George cut the branch, so he
- A. gasped
- B. called Frau Carver
- C. went back to work
- D. shouted

_____ 9. Frau Carver looked at the cut branch and saw
- A. insects
- B. the ax
- C. buds
- D. an apple

_____ 10. This story is about the childhood of
- A. Farmer Carver
- B. George W. Carver
- C. George Washington
- D. Frau Carver

© Steck-Vaughn Company

Name ________________________ Date ____________

Yoshiko Uchida

Read the story. Choose the answer that best completes each sentence.

The California sun streamed in the window. Yoshiko gazed at her mother's face. Her mother was a poet. She was reading a *tanka*. A tanka is a Japanese poem with 31 syllables. Yoshiko listened to the calm voice. She closed her eyes. She did not want to miss a single beat of the verse.

Yoshiko's parents had grown up in Japan. They had moved to California before Yoshiko was born. They wanted her to know about the Japanese culture. So her family read Japanese stories and books. They wrote and received letters from Japan. Guests from Japan came to their home. When she was ten, Yoshiko began writing her own stories. These stories marked the start of her life as a writer.

_____ 1. Yoshiko and her parents lived in
- A. Japan
- B. California
- C. Boston
- D. Tokyo

_____ 2. Yoshiko's mother was a
- A. cook
- B. doctor
- C. musician
- D. poet

_____ 3. A tanka is a special
- A. story
- B. song
- C. poem
- D. letter

_____ 4. Yoshiko learned about Japan from
- A. television
- B. school
- C. her parents
- D. a neighbor

_____ 5. Yoshiko wrote her first stories when she was
- A. ten
- B. twelve
- C. fifteen
- D. twenty

Go on to the next page.

© Steck-Vaughn Company

Name ______________________________________ Date ____________________

Yoshiko's work reflects her life as a Japanese American. Her first book, *The Dancing Kettle*, retells some folk tales of Japan. She thinks that folk tales tell about feelings that all humans share. She hopes the tales will help people see that they have many of the same hopes and fears.

Yoshiko has written many other stories. Some are picture books for young children. Another tells about the first settlers from Japan. Other books tell about growing up in California. These are titled *A Jar of Dreams* and *The Best Bad Thing*.

Yoshiko's books give today's young Japanese Americans something new. It is something that she did not have when she was young. Few people had written books about being Japanese in America. Her books are among the first that blend the two cultures.

_____ **6.** Yoshiko's first book is called
- **A.** *The First Settlers*
- **B.** *The Dancing Kettle*
- **C.** *The Best Bad Thing*
- **D.** *A Jar of Dreams*

_____ **7.** Yoshiko thinks that folk tales tell about
- **A.** feelings
- **B.** settlers
- **C.** growing up
- **D.** Japan

_____ **8.** Yoshiko has written
- **A.** a comedy
- **B.** a journal
- **C.** a picture book
- **D.** for the newspaper

_____ **9.** Yoshiko wrote about
- **A.** Japanese Americans
- **B.** young girls
- **C.** famous writers
- **D.** Californians

_____ **10.** Books about the blending of two cultures are
- **A.** common
- **B.** hard
- **C.** old
- **D.** new

© Steck-Vaughn Company

Name ________________________________ Date ______________

The Mountain of Ice

At dawn the sunlight falls on the Andes Mountains of Ecuador. The light shines on Chimborazo, the highest peak. Centuries ago Chimborazo was an active volcano. Hot lava poured from its mouth. Now the lava has hardened into rocks. Great sheets of ice are mixed in with the rocks. The upper slopes of the mountain are so cold that the ice stays there all year.

Once a week a small group of people get ready to climb Chimborazo. The men are ice miners. They load axes and other tools onto the backs of a dozen donkeys.

At the foot of the great mountain, the miners stop for a while. They gather bundles of long grasses and load them onto the donkeys, too. Then the men and animals begin to climb. They must go up to 18,500 feet, and the journey takes at least five hours.

When they reach the ice fields, the miners go to work. It isn't easy to chop the thick ice away from the heavy rocks. The miners cut the ice out in blocks that weigh about twenty pounds each. Then they wrap the ice blocks in grass and put them on the donkeys' backs. Each donkey can carry two or three of these blocks. The men and their animals head down the mountain. By the time they reach home, it is night.

The next day the miners take the ice to town. The miners sell each block of ice for about twenty cents to the people who make snow cones. Thirsty shoppers buy the snow cones in the market.

Ice is rare in town because there are no refrigerators or freezers. That's why the ice miners are always welcome at the market. The next week, just before market day, the miners will once more make the long trip to the cold peak of Chimborazo.

Go on to the next page.

© Steck-Vaughn Company

Name ______________________________ Date ________________

1. Put these events in the order that they happened. What happened first? Write the number **1** on the line by that sentence. Then write the number **2** by the sentence that tells what happened next. Write the number **3** by the sentence that tells what happened last.

_____ The miners cut ice into blocks.

_____ The miners climb Chimborazo.

_____ The miners load axes on the donkeys.

Choose the phrase that best answers the question.

_____ 2. When do the miners gather bundles of grass?

A. before they reach the ice fields
B. before they load the axes
C. after they wrap the ice blocks

_____ 3. When do the miners climb the mountain?

A. every morning
B. once a week
C. during market day

_____ 4. When do the miners come home from the mountain?

A. by the time night comes
B. on market day
C. the next morning

_____ 5. When did lava pour from Chimborazo?

A. on market day
B. long ago
C. every week

© Steck-Vaughn Company

Name ______________________ Date ______________

Urban Man

If you've ever been to a zoo, you've probably seen some very unusual sights. Visitors saw a strange sight at the MetroZoo in Miami, Florida.

The zoo was new. It had 225 acres of land. It had many types of animals wandering around the grounds. It also had a small lake and a miniature golf course. Still, the zoo did not have as many visitors as it needed. If the zoo had more visitors, it would make more money. The zoo needed this money to take care of its animals and their homes. So the zoo opened a new exhibit. It was called Urban Man. The sign near the exhibit read: "Found in cities throughout the planet."

People were curious. They came by the dozens to see Urban Man. He was in a cage with some giant turtles. He had on a dark suit, a white shirt, and a tie. He carried a briefcase.

As people stared, Urban Man got ready for the day. He brushed his teeth. Then he shaved. When he was finished, he ate his breakfast. While he ate, he read the morning newspaper.

Then Urban Man got up and walked around. He did not speak, but he did hand out his business cards. The cards read, "Urban Man." The children in the crowd pushed nearer so they could get one.

After that Urban Man went to his big desk. He shuffled some of the papers on it. The zoo visitors thought that was wonderful. Later on in the day, Urban Man used some of his machines. He listened to music on his stereo and watched a program on his television.

Urban Man was a big success. However, he was only at the zoo for 72 hours. After that he picked up his paycheck and left. In real life *this* Urban Man was an actor. Working in the zoo was just one of the parts he played.

Go on to the next page.

Name ________________________________ Date ________________

1. Put these events in the order that they happened. What happened first? Write the number **1** on the line by that sentence. Then write the number **2** by the sentence that tells what happened next. Write the number **3** by the sentence that tells what happened last.

_____ People came to see Urban Man.

_____ The zoo did not have many visitors.

_____ The zoo opened a new exhibit.

Choose the phrase that best answers the question.

_____ **2.** When did Urban Man get his paycheck?

- **A.** at the end of the day
- **B.** after 72 hours
- **C.** at breakfast time

_____ **3.** When did Urban Man eat breakfast?

- **A.** while he read the paper
- **B.** after he listened to his stereo
- **C.** while he brushed his teeth

_____ **4.** When did Urban Man walk around?

- **A.** while he read the morning paper
- **B.** after he ate breakfast
- **C.** before he went to bed

_____ **5.** When did the Urban Man exhibit open?

- **A.** after Urban Man left
- **B.** while Urban Man brushed his teeth
- **C.** when MetroZoo was new

© Steck-Vaughn Company

Name ________________________________ Date ________________

Football Factory

A football has to be tough. After all, it gets kicked around most of the time. So each football is made very carefully. It takes about fifty steps to make a football.

It all starts with leather. About two feet of leather are needed to cover a pro football. A machine cuts the leather into four pieces. Another machine stamps the pieces. The stamp tells the name of the company that makes the ball. Workers then sew a cloth lining to each piece. Next they stitch the four pieces together. A small opening is left. The football is then turned inside out. Workers trim the extra leather inside.

The football is turned right side out again. A worker puts a rubber lining into the ball. Now the opening in the ball is sewed up. Each ball is sewed three times by hand. The first time, a worker uses heavy linen thread to close the opening. After that, two sets of leather laces are added. These laces help players get a good grip on the ball.

Once the ball is sewed up, it is placed on an iron mold. A worker pumps air into the rubber lining. Then another worker shines the leather football.

Next, workers weigh and measure the ball to see that it is the right size and the right weight. A football should weigh between 14 and 15 ounces. It should be 21 inches around and 11 inches from end to end. A good football must be strong so it stands up to rough play. But it must not be too hard or players will hurt their feet when they kick it.

If the football is just right, it goes to the packing area. Workers then put the balls in boxes to send to professional teams and sports stores.

Go on to the next page.

Name ______________________________ Date ______________

1. Put these events in the order that they happened. What happened first? Write the number **1** on the line by that sentence. Then write the number **2** by the sentence that tells what happened next. Write the number **3** by the sentence that tells what happened last.

_____ Machines cut pieces from leather.

_____ Workers sew in a cloth lining.

_____ Machines stamp the leather pieces.

Choose the phrase that best answers the question.

_____ **2.** When are the four pieces sewed together?

A. while a worker sews in a cloth lining
B. before the inside is trimmed
C. after workers check the ball's weight

_____ **3.** When is a rubber lining put into the football?

A. while the ball is turned inside out
B. after the ball is turned right side out
C. before the ball is turned inside out

_____ **4.** When is each ball sewed up with leather laces?

A. before the rubber lining is added
B. while the lining is added
C. after it is sewed with linen thread

_____ **5.** When are the footballs measured?

A. after they are sent to stores
B. while they are inspected
C. while they are used in games

Name ______________________________ Date ______________

Kind Taxi Driver

It's easy to lose things in a big city. So finding lost things can be a special event.

One day in August of 1985, a photographer lost some film in New York City. The photographer had just returned from the West Coast. She had taken 25 rolls of film on her trip. Just before she got on the airplane, she took the film out of her camera bag. She put it in a clear bag. That way the people at the airport could check it. The film would not have to go through the x-ray machine. Sometimes x-ray machines destroy film.

After the photographer's plane landed, she got in a taxi. She put her bags on the seat and told the driver her address. Soon they pulled up to her apartment. The photographer paid the driver and left the taxi. But she forgot her bag of film.

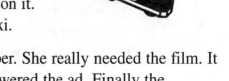

It didn't take her long to realize what she had done. But it was too late. The taxi was gone, and the bag had no name on it. The photographer did not even know the number of the taxi.

The next day the photographer put an ad in the newspaper. She really needed the film. It represented quite a bit of work. Days went by. No one answered the ad. Finally the photographer gave up.

Four months passed. The photographer was in another part of the city. She called a taxi to take her home. When the taxi driver got to her apartment, he said, "I've been here before. Did you happen to lose some film last August?"

The photographer hugged the driver. He had all 25 rolls of her film. They were in perfect shape. His next passenger had found the film. The taxi driver had then gone back to the photographer's building. But he didn't know her name, and he couldn't find her. So he had driven around with the film ever since. He knew it was rare to pick up the same passenger twice in New York. But it wasn't impossible!

Go on to the next page.

© Steck-Vaughn Company

Name ______________________________ Date ________________

1. Put these events in the order that they happened. What happened first? Write the number **1** on the line by that sentence. Then write the number **2** by the sentence that tells what happened next. Write the number **3** by the sentence that tells what happened last.

_____ The photographer landed in New York.

_____ The photographer put the film in a clear bag.

_____ The photographer got in a taxi.

Choose the phrase that best answers the question.

_____ **2.** When did the photographer put the film in a bag?

A. while she was on the plane
B. before she got on the plane
C. after the plane landed

_____ **3.** When did the photographer realize her film was gone?

A. after she left the taxi
B. before she left the airport
C. while she was in the taxi

_____ **4.** When did the photographer get the film back?

A. after four days
B. in August
C. after four months

_____ **5.** When did the taxi driver read the ad in the newspaper?

A. never
B. August of 1985
C. after the photographer wrote the ad

© Steck-Vaughn Company

Name ______________________________ Date ______________

Lost in the Yukon

Helen Klaben was the only passenger on the small plane that was flying from Alaska to Washington. She stared out the window at the swirling, white snowstorm. It was February 4, 1963. Ralph Flores, the pilot of the plane, wasn't sure whether or not they were still on course. He dropped to a lower altitude to see better. He glanced down to change gas tanks. A moment later the plane crashed into some trees.

Both Helen and Ralph were hurt in the crash. Several of Ralph's ribs were broken and so was his jaw. Helen's left arm was broken. Her feet became so frostbitten that she could barely walk. It was 48 degrees below zero. They had little food and no sleeping bags. Both of them knew how serious their situation was. They were frightened but determined to survive.

Helen rested in the plane most of the time. Ralph kept himself busy. He built fires and worked on the plane's radio. He flashed mirrors and made a trap to catch rabbits.

By the tenth day, they had run out of food. On the fortieth day, they knew that no one would find them in the forest. They would have to leave the plane and find a large clearing. Maybe then a passing plane would see them. It was their only chance!

Ralph made a sled for Helen. He pulled her through the deep snow until they finally reached a meadow. There they built a shelter from tree branches. But after a few days, Ralph decided that the clearing wasn't big enough. Four miles away, he found a larger meadow. He spent the next three days stamping out *SOS* in 70-foot letters.

On March 24 a pilot saw the *SOS*. Forty-nine days after the crash, Helen and Ralph were finally rescued. Rescue workers knew that only people with a great will to live could have survived for so long.

Go on to the next page.

© Steck-Vaughn Company

Name ______________________________ Date ______________

1. Put these events in the order that they happened. What happened first? Write the number **1** on the line by that sentence. Then write the number **2** by the sentence that tells what happened next. Write the number **3** by the sentence that tells what happened last.

_____ The plane crashed into some trees.

_____ Ralph looked down to change gas tanks.

_____ Helen's feet were badly frostbitten.

Choose the phrase that best answers the question.

_____ **2.** When did Ralph work on the plane's radio?

- **A.** before the plane wreck
- **B.** on the fortieth day
- **C.** while they were using the plane as shelter

_____ **3.** When did they run out of food?

- **A.** before February 4
- **B.** on the tenth day after they crashed
- **C.** after March 24

_____ **4.** When did they leave the plane to look for a clearing?

- **A.** about 40 days after the plane wreck
- **B.** soon after the plane wreck
- **C.** on March 24

_____ **5.** When were Helen and Ralph rescued?

- **A.** 49 days after the crash
- **B.** on February 4
- **C.** 10 days after the crash

© Steck-Vaughn Company

Name ______________________ Date ______________

Maple Syrup

Have you ever had maple syrup on your pancakes or waffles? Did you know it is the sap of a tree? For years it was the only sweetener that Native Americans and settlers used. Today maple syrup is made in the northeastern part of the United States.

Let's follow one Vermont farm family as they harvest the sap from their maple trees. Each March the Browns watch the weather carefully. When it is just right, they know that the sap is running. It is time to put tapholes in the trees. They load equipment on a sled. Two horses pull the sled through the snow to the maple trees.

First, one and one-half-inch holes are drilled in the trees. Then metal spouts are hammered into the holes. Each spout has a hook that holds a bucket. Buckets are hung on the spouts, and lids are placed over them.

The next day the Browns get the sled ready to gather the sap that has dripped out of the trees. They load a huge tank on the sled. Gathering is stop-and-go work. The sap is emptied into big buckets. When those buckets are full, they are poured into the big tank on the sled. When all the trees have been visited, the Browns head for the sugarhouse. They store the sap there.

The Browns gather the sap each day, until it quits running. Then it is time to make syrup. The sap is mainly water. The water must be boiled off so the syrup will be thick and sweet. The Browns build a big fire in the sugarhouse. The sap is poured into evaporator pans that hang above the fire.

The heat turns the sap into syrup. When it is finally ready, the syrup drains into buckets. It is now a sweet, golden liquid. The Browns will have enough maple syrup for the rest of the year. They will celebrate the next morning with a pancake breakfast.

Go on to the next page.

© Steck-Vaughn Company

Name ________________________________ Date ________________

1. Put these events in the order that they happened. What happened first? Write the number **1** on the line by that sentence. Then write the number **2** by the sentence that tells what happened next. Write the number **3** by the sentence that tells what happened last.

_____ The sap is stored in the sugarhouse.

_____ The sap is boiled.

_____ The sap begins to run.

Choose the phrase that best answers the question.

_____ **2.** When does the sap run?

A. during the summer
B. usually in March
C. while it is boiling

_____ **3.** When are metal spouts hammered into the trees?

A. after the tapholes are drilled
B. during the fall
C. after the buckets are hung on the trees

_____ **4.** How often is the sap gathered?

A. every two weeks
B. every Monday
C. each day, until it quits running

_____ **5.** When does maple sap turn into syrup?

A. when the water is boiled off
B. when it is poured over pancakes
C. when the buckets are hung on the trees

© Steck-Vaughn Company

Name ______________________________ Date ______________

Koalas

Koalas are sometimes called koala bears because they look like live teddy bears. But koalas aren't bears. They are marsupials. Marsupials are mammals with pouches. Most marsupials live in Australia. If you lived in Australia, you could go to a koala preserve and see these cute, cuddly animals for yourself.

After mating, a female koala waits for about five weeks. Then her tiny, blind baby is born. The hairless baby is about three fourths of an inch long. It looks like a worm with a big head and arms. The baby koala must climb six inches to get into its mother's pouch. This is a dangerous journey. If the tiny koala falls off, it will die.

The baby is safe once it's inside the mother's pouch. A strong muscle keeps the pouch closed for the first few months. The baby has plenty to eat. It grows larger, and its fur becomes thick. From time to time, it sticks its head out and looks around.

The baby stays in the pouch for about six months. Then it is ready to come out for short periods of time. By now it is seven inches long and has its first teeth. The baby chews on young gum leaves, as well as drinking its mother's milk.

After leaving the pouch, the koala baby rides on its mother's back. The mother's strong arms and claws allow her to climb easily, even with the baby on her back. For the next few months, the baby clings to its mother during the day. But at night it returns to the pouch. At about nine months old, the young koala will go short distances from the mother to eat gum leaves by itself.

The mother koala takes good care of her baby for about a year. By then the baby is full grown and can take care of itself.

Go on to the next page.

© Steck-Vaughn Company

Name ______________________________ Date ________________

1. Put these events in the order that they happened. What happened first? Write the number **1** on the line by that sentence. Then write the number **2** by the sentence that tells what happened next. Write the number **3** by the sentence that tells what happened last.

_____ The baby koala stays in the pouch for six months.

_____ The tiny, blind baby is born.

_____ The baby koala rides on its mother's back.

Choose the phrase that best answers the question.

_____ **2.** When does the baby koala look like a worm?

- **A.** when it's about six months old
- **B.** after it's a year old
- **C.** when it's born

_____ **3.** When does the baby koala make a dangerous journey?

- **A.** when it first tries to reach its mother's pouch
- **B.** the first time it climbs a tree
- **C.** when it's 18 months old

_____ **4.** When does the baby koala first leave the pouch?

- **A.** before it's five weeks old
- **B.** when it's about six months old
- **C.** after it's full grown

_____ **5.** How long does a mother koala care for her baby?

- **A.** about one year
- **B.** less than six weeks
- **C.** more than three years

© Steck-Vaughn Company

Name ______________________________ Date ______________

Read the story. Choose the word that best completes each sentence.

Most auroras appear high in the far northern and southern night skies. They are __(1)__ streaks of colored lights. Green is the most __(2)__ color, but red and purple are often seen.

_____ **1.** **A.** anxious **B.** spectacular **C.** low **D.** painted

_____ **2.** **A.** common **B.** even **C.** difficult **D.** unlikely

---

Computers are fun and __(3)__ machines. They help us store and work with information. Some people use them to __(4)__ math problems. Others like them just for playing games.

_____ **3.** **A.** lazy **B.** helpless **C.** useful **D.** awkward

_____ **4.** **A.** earn **B.** solve **C.** refuse **D.** destroy

---

The cheetah is a big cat. It is known for its great speed as it runs short __(5)__ . It uses its sleek body and long, powerful legs to run fast. This cat's claws help it grab the ground as it races to catch its __(6)__ .

_____ **5.** **A.** days **B.** evenings **C.** naps **D.** stretches

_____ **6.** **A.** bath **B.** water **C.** quarry **D.** apple

---

Fossils are the traces or remains of living things from millions of years ago. They include shells, bones, and teeth that have been __(7)__ in rocks. Petrified wood and dinosaur tracks are also fossil __(8)__ .

_____ **7.** **A.** retained **B.** grown **C.** sold **D.** thrown

_____ **8.** **A.** rows **B.** specimens **C.** echoes **D.** names

Go on to the next page.

Name ______________________________ Date ______________

Read the story. Choose the word that best completes the sentence.

Some mushrooms are good to eat. But others are **toxic**. Often an expert is the only one who can tell them apart. You can stay safe by buying your mushrooms from a store.

_____ **9.** In this paragraph, the word **toxic** means

A. fruit **C.** delicious

B. crisp **D.** poisonous

A tornado is a very **fierce** storm. This funnel-shaped cloud does not last long. But it sucks up everything in its path. The strong winds can be very destructive.

_____ **10.** In this paragraph, the word **fierce** means

A. friendly **C.** dangerous

B. sticky **D.** small

The stonefish lives in the ocean waters of Australia. It is well **camouflaged** because it looks like a stone. If a stonefish is stepped on, the poison from its spines can cause death.

_____ **11.** In this paragraph, the word **camouflaged** means

A. detailed **C.** appeared

B. hidden **D.** exercised

Mark Wellman wanted to climb El Capitán in California. He is physically disabled. He knew climbing this rock wall wouldn't be easy. He pulled himself up most of the way. Then a friend carried him to the **summit**. Mark had found a way up.

_____ **12.** In this paragraph, the word **summit** means

A. peak **C.** side

B. quarrel **D.** bottom

© Steck-Vaughn Company

Name ______________________________ Date ______________

Read the story. Choose the word that best completes each sentence.

The castle was once a very important place, and it had many uses. It was a palace for the rulers of the region. Lawbreakers were held in a __(1)__ that was part of the castle. The castle also served as a __(2)__ for protection against enemies.

_____ **1.** **A.** tree **B.** prison **C.** closet **D.** window

_____ **2.** **A.** fort **B.** curtain **C.** ranch **D.** harvest

---

At a __(3)__ you will see the water level rise and fall twice each day. The tides change like this because the moon and the sun pull on the earth. This pull is known as gravity. It forces the surface of the sea to pull up __(4)__ toward the moon or the sun.

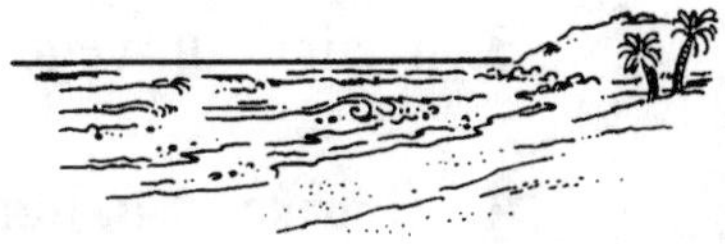

_____ **3.** **A.** shoreline **B.** fair **C.** debate **D.** theater

_____ **4.** **A.** poorly **B.** timely **C.** freshly **D.** slightly

---

Although a koala looks similar to a bear, in __(5)__ it is not a bear at all. This cute, cuddly __(6)__ is a marsupial. This means a mother koala will carry her baby in a pouch as it grows.

_____ **5.** **A.** object **B.** fact **C.** arm **D.** hunger

_____ **6.** **A.** bear **B.** insect **C.** creature **D.** savage

---

Stonehenge is a circle of huge stones. It stands on a flat __(7)__ in England. It was __(8)__ more than four thousand years ago. It may have been used for measuring time. But there are still many questions about how and why it was built.

_____ **7.** **A.** hug **B.** plain **C.** river **D.** carpet

_____ **8.** **A.** delayed **B.** taught **C.** chased **D.** erected

Name ______________________________ Date ______________

Read the story. Choose the word that best completes each sentence.

Each of your eyes sees things a bit differently. Your brain ___(1)___ the two pictures so you see only one. Sometimes you can ___(2)___ a picture in more than one way. Your eyes are tricked into seeing slightly different pictures. When this occurs, your brain gets confused. This is called an optical illusion.

_____ **1.** **A.** faces **B.** reports **C.** dims **D.** blends

_____ **2.** **A.** hold **B.** interpret **C.** remove **D.** draw

---

An oasis is an area of lush green ___(3)___ in a desert. It exists because there is water under the ground. When the water lies close to the surface, an oasis can ___(4)___ .

_____ **3.** **A.** air **B.** vegetation **C.** jail **D.** harp

_____ **4.** **A.** arise **B.** hurry **C.** fit **D.** drown

---

You know that calculators are well ___(5)___ because so many people use them. But this was not always the case. Calculators have gone through many ___(6)___ . At first, calculators were large and solved problems slowly. Today they are much smaller and can compute problems quickly.

_____ **5.** **A.** launched **B.** poured **C.** accepted **D.** won

_____ **6.** **A.** keys **B.** books **C.** parts **D.** stages

---

Agatha Christie wrote about solving strange ___(7)___ . One night she drove off and disappeared. Two weeks later the police found Agatha staying at a hotel. She couldn't recall what had happened. She claimed to have lost her ___(8)___ .

_____ **7.** **A.** crimes **B.** plants **C.** maps **D.** boxes

_____ **8.** **A.** car **B.** memory **C.** glasses **D.** watch

© Steck-Vaughn Company

Name ________________________________ Date ______________

Read the story. Choose the word that best completes each sentence.

A sea horse is a tiny fish with a long tail. Its head looks like that of a horse. It moves by swimming upright. The sea horse has a single fin on its back that __(1)__ it through the water. If the sea horse wants to stop, it __(2)__ its tail around a sea plant.

_____ **1.** **A.** lives **B.** propels **C.** sings **D.** feeds

_____ **2.** **A.** coils **B.** loses **C.** hits **D.** plants

---

Geckos are lizards that are good climbers. There are more than eight hundred varieties of geckos. Many of them make clicking __(3)__ with their tongues. Others are __(4)__ and never make any noise.

_____ **3.** **A.** eyes **B.** bites **C.** sounds **D.** leaps

_____ **4.** **A.** tan **B.** tired **C.** nervous **D.** silent

---

There are huge drawings in the desert of Peru. Many are so big that you wouldn't be able to tell what they were if you were standing on the ground. The drawings can be recognized only when __(5)__ from high above. The Nazca Indians drew these __(6)__ many years ago. The reason they were drawn and how they were used is not known.

_____ **5.** **A.** heard **B.** sent **C.** viewed **D.** trapped

_____ **6.** **A.** causes **B.** jobs **C.** designs **D.** reports

---

Wind power is an old __(7)__ of energy. The windmills used now are much better than they once were. Windmills can supply __(8)__ power to run lights, toasters, fans, and radios in homes.

_____ **7.** **A.** plan **B.** job **C.** trick **D.** sort

_____ **8.** **A.** wave **B.** electrical **C.** circus **D.** no

© Steck-Vaughn Company

Name ______________________________ Date ______________

Read the story. Choose the word that best completes each sentence.

Franklin Chang-Diaz made a big __(1)__ . He set a goal of flying in space. He trained as a pilot and a scientist. Then Franklin learned how to __(2)__ the space shuttle. In 1986 he achieved his goal when he went on a mission in the space shuttle *Columbia*.

_____ **1.** **A.** decision **B.** nest **C.** door **D.** hand

_____ **2.** **A.** reward **B.** hide **C.** locate **D.** operate

---

Flying squirrels have flaps of skin between their hind and front legs. These flaps can be used like a parachute. The squirrels leap from high branches and __(3)__ their flaps of skin. Then they __(4)__ through the air to lower branches.

_____ **3.** **A.** tear **B.** wrinkle **C.** spread **D.** forget

_____ **4.** **A.** trot **B.** soar **C.** freeze **D.** look

---

In 1908 a large crash was heard in a Siberian forest. The cause for this must have been very __(5)__ . It knocked down trees for miles. The fallen trees all pointed outward in a huge circle. People thought it was a meteor, but there was no __(6)__ in the ground.

_____ **5.** **A.** weak **B.** powerful **C.** helpful **D.** quiet

_____ **6.** **A.** crater **B.** soil **C.** water **D.** tool

---

A hedgehog is an unusual animal. It snorts as it __(7)__ for food at night. If it senses danger, the hedgehog will roll into a ball with its spines pointed out. During the day it stays safe in its nest. Sometimes it will __(8)__ loudly as it sleeps.

_____ **7.** **A.** eats **B.** rummages **C.** melts **D.** dresses

_____ **8.** **A.** type **B.** march **C.** snore **D.** eat

© Steck-Vaughn Company

Name ______________________________ Date ______________

Read the story. Choose the word that best completes each sentence.

Texans fought a war to become free. A Hispanic woman, Andrea Castañon Ramirez Candalária, was a nurse. She worked at a Texas mission __(1)__ the Alamo. She __(2)__ for the injured men. Andrea was wounded in the war, but she survived. She lived to be 113 years old.

_____ 1. A. called B. carved C. stored D. won

_____ 2. A. held B. cared C. asked D. touched

A sponge lives at the bottom of the sea. A sponge will not die if it is cut into __(3)__ . Each section will grow new body parts. A sponge's body __(4)__ many holes. Water takes air and food through these holes.

_____ 3. A. animals B. bins C. pieces D. stories

_____ 4. A. rewards B. contains C. eats D. whispers

The international date line helps us keep up with dates around the world. This is __(5)__ since the earth's spin makes midnight, the start of a new day, occur at different times in different places. You can take a __(6)__ around the world. You lose a day going west and gain a day going east.

_____ 5. A. careless B. told C. calm D. essential

_____ 6. A. stone B. trip C. glove D. clap

Falling objects are pulled down by gravity. A parachute slows down this fall. In an __(7)__ a person safely jumps from a plane using a parachute. __(8)__ such as food can also be easily dropped.

_____ 7. A. acre B. issue C. emergency D. empty

_____ 8. A. Goods B. News C. Water D. Facts

© Steck-Vaughn Company

Name ______________________ Date ______________

Read the story. Choose the word that best completes each sentence.

Satellites have been sent into space to __(1)__ the earth. They have been made for different __(2)__ . Some satellites help us communicate with other people in the world. Others help us study the weather or changes on the earth's surface.

_____ **1.** **A.** fix **B.** turn **C.** enter **D.** orbit

_____ **2.** **A.** models **B.** reasons **C.** acts **D.** traps

In 1910 Madame C. J. Walker __(3)__ a line of cosmetic products. As her __(4)__ grew, she started many beauty schools. She was the first African-American woman to become a millionaire.

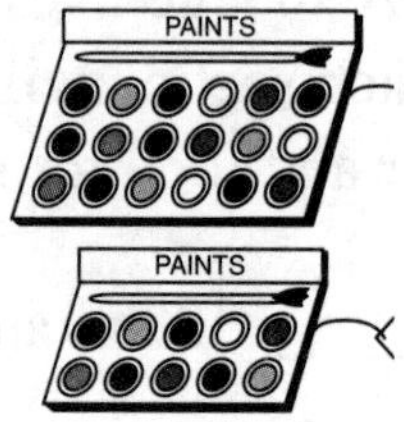

_____ **3.** **A.** helped **B.** napped **C.** manufactured **D.** piled

_____ **4.** **A.** business **B.** appetite **C.** show **D.** comfort

In 1520 Ferdinand Magellan set a __(5)__ to find the Pacific. As he searched, he sailed to the southern end of South America. There Magellan saw a group of islands. Large fires burned on the shores. He named the __(6)__ Tierra del Fuego, or Land of Fire.

_____ **5.** **A.** course **B.** fort **C.** bird **D.** child

_____ **6.** **A.** face **B.** region **C.** task **D.** minute

There's an old tale about a large island. It is said to have been located in the Atlantic Ocean. This island was called Atlantis. A strong __(7)__ ruled the island. Its armies tried to conquer both Greece and Egypt, but they lost. Later this island sank due to volcanic eruptions, earthquakes, and __(8)__ from a tidal wave.

_____ **7.** **A.** statue **B.** building **C.** chat **D.** empire

_____ **8.** **A.** news **B.** tracks **C.** floods **D.** avenues

© Steck-Vaughn Company

Name ______________________________ Date ________________

Read the story. Choose the word that best completes the sentence.

Most people like football because it is full of action. But the ball is in motion only twenty percent of the game. The rest of the time is **expended** in things such as huddles and time-outs.

_____ **1.** In this paragraph, the word **expended** means

A. kicked C. wished

B. spent D. saved

Many towns in our country have **quaint** names. Some odd ones are Darling, Lemon, and Soso in Mississippi. The town of Licking is in Ohio. And you'll find Snowflake in Arizona.

_____ **2.** In this paragraph, the word **quaint** means

A. unusual C. southern

B. long D. regular

The squid is a sea animal with ten **tentacles**. It uses eight of them to catch its food. The other two are longer. The squid uses them to bring the food to its mouth.

_____ **3.** In this paragraph, the word **tentacles** means

A. eyes C. nets

B. arms D. heads

The deepest lake in the world is found in Russia. It is more than five thousand feet deep. Its great depth **surpasses** the height of some mountains.

_____ **4.** In this paragraph, the word **surpasses** means

A. shines above C. appears

B. loses D. goes beyond

© Steck-Vaughn Company

Name ______________________________ Date ______________

Read the story. Choose the word that best completes the sentence.

You know that a deck of cards has 52 cards. Did you know that if you put the names of all the cards together, you will have **precisely** 52 letters? Write out the names, add up the letters, and the sum will be 52.

_____ **1.** In this paragraph, the word **precisely** means

A. above C. exactly
B. under D. over

The rose has long been a sign of **secrecy**. Hundreds of years ago, people wore roses behind their ears. It meant that the people wearing the roses had heard something, but would not tell what they had heard.

_____ **2.** In this paragraph, the word **secrecy** means

A. riddles C. talking
B. silence D. sharing

Paul Cézanne was a famous French painter. It is said that he worked very slowly. Since one of his favorite subjects was fruit, it often **perished** before he finished. So Cézanne began painting fruit made of wax instead.

_____ **3.** In this paragraph, the word **perished** means

A. spoiled C. fell
B. ate D. grew

Suppose you are at a typewriter. What word can you type with only the top row of letters? **Ponder** the problem no further. You can type *typewriter*!

_____ **4.** In this paragraph, the word **ponder** means

A. strike C. forget
B. think about D. know of

© Steck-Vaughn Company

Name ______________________________ Date ______________

Read the story. Choose the word that best completes the sentence.

There is only one flock of whooping cranes in the world. These **endangered** birds live in Canada. They migrate to Texas for the winter. If all the birds in this flock die, the whooping crane will become extinct.

_____ **1.** In this paragraph, the word **endangered** means

- **A.** large
- **B.** white
- **C.** threatened
- **D.** Canadian

France and England were at war from 1337 to 1453. This war is called the Hundred Years' War although it **endured** for 116 years. The war was finally won by France.

_____ **2.** In this paragraph, the word **endured** means

- **A.** was won
- **B.** injured
- **C.** ended
- **D.** lasted

Echo talked too much. So, she was **forbidden** to speak without first being spoken to. She could only repeat what she heard.

_____ **3.** In this paragraph, the word **forbidden** means

- **A.** loud
- **B.** whispered
- **C.** encouraged to
- **D.** prevented from

On the tip of each finger is a pattern of ridges. This pattern is called a fingerprint. Each finger has a **distinct** fingerprint. No two people in the world have the same fingerprints. A person's fingerprints always remain the same—they never change.

_____ **4.** In this paragraph, the word **distinct** means

- **A.** particular
- **B.** silver
- **C.** smooth
- **D.** funny

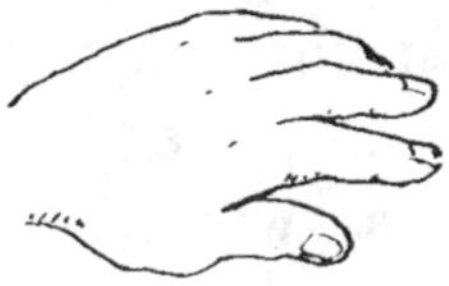

© Steck-Vaughn Company

Name ________________________________ Date ______________

Read the story. Choose the word that best completes the sentence.

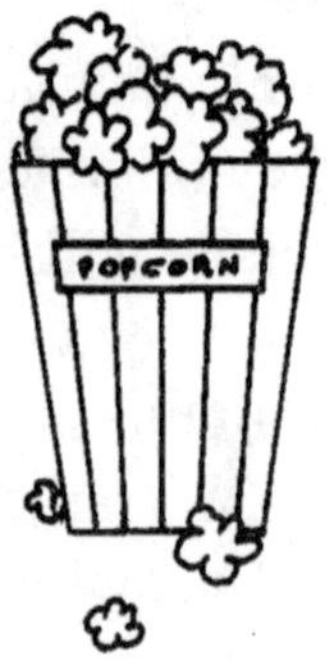

What makes popcorn pop? Popcorn kernels are small and hard. There is water within the kernel. When the moisture heats up, it turns to steam. The **steam** causes the kernel to explode.

_____ **1.** In this paragraph, the word **steam** means

A. dry corn **C.** melted butter

B. hot air **D.** sea salt

Many people believe that red makes a bull angry and causes him to attack. That is why a bullfighter waves a red cape. But a bull is colorblind. It is the **motion** of the cape that excites the bull. A bullfighter could wave a white or green cape, and the bull would charge.

_____ **2.** In this paragraph, the word **motion** means

A. color **C.** stopping

B. red **D.** shaking

Only one bird can fly **backward**. It is the tiny hummingbird. The bird flies in front of a flower. It sucks the nectar out of the flower. When it is finished, it simply backs up.

_____ **3.** In this paragraph, the word **backward** means

A. in reverse **C.** up and down

B. fast **D.** like a helicopter

In shot-putting, the shot used by men weighs 16 pounds. The one used by women weighs 9 pounds. Each **competitor** throws the shot from a circle to a special landing area. The winner is the one who throws the shot the farthest.

_____ **4.** In this paragraph, the word **competitor** means

A. player **C.** audience

B. winner **D.** special equipment

© Steck-Vaughn Company

Name ________________________________ Date ______________

Read the story. Choose the word that best completes the sentence.

Lorraine Hansberry wrote the play *A Raisin in the Sun.* It is about an African-American family that wants to **relocate** to a white neighborhood. The move brings out the love and strength in the family. *A Raisin in the Sun* was the first play on Broadway written by an African-American woman.

_____ **1.** In this paragraph, the word **relocate** means

A. visit
B. write a play
C. move to a new place
D. stay away from

Colorado got its name from a Spanish word. The Spanish word *colorado* means "red." Spanish explorers found a river with reddish-colored water. They **declared** it the Colorado River. The state got its name from the river.

_____ **2.** In this paragraph, the word **declared** means

A. swam in
B. colored
C. discovered
D. made it known as

Albert Von Tilzer must have been very **creative**. He wrote the song "Take Me Out to the Ball Game." But Albert had never been to a baseball game. He did not even like the sport! He wrote the song by thinking about how much fun a game might be.

_____ **3.** In this paragraph, the word **creative** means

A. dull
B. athletic
C. a baseball fan
D. able to imagine

Mistletoe has thick green leaves and white berries. It is never found growing on the ground. This plant does not grow in soil. It grows on the **limbs** of trees.

_____ **4.** In this paragraph, the word **limbs** means

A. clouds
B. branches
C. roots
D. flowers

© Steck-Vaughn Company

Name ________________________ Date ____________

Read the story. Choose the word that best completes the sentence.

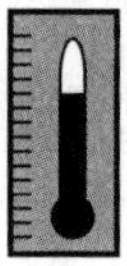

Mercury is a metal that stays liquid whether it is hot or cold. Mercury is used inside a **thermometer**. It can show if you are running a fever.

_____ **1.** In this paragraph, the word **thermometer** means
- **A.** cleans teeth
- **B.** weeds gardens
- **C.** measures hot and cold
- **D.** loses weight

Sometimes it looks as if there is a ring of light shining around the moon. This is **actually** from clouds high in the earth's atmosphere. The clouds have bits of ice that bend and scatter the moonlight. This is usually a sign that a storm is coming.

_____ **2.** In this paragraph, the word **actually** means
- **A.** suddenly
- **B.** really
- **C.** exactly
- **D.** quickly

The black mamba is a snake. It lives in Africa. The mamba has a bad temper and will attack if it is disturbed. A very small amount of its venom can be **fatal** to a person.

_____ **3.** In this paragraph, the word **fatal** means
- **A.** causing death
- **B.** making wrong
- **C.** getting well
- **D.** seeming happy

Koko, a gorilla, was taught how to communicate using sign language. She asked for a kitten for her birthday. Koko carefully **attended** to her kitten. She talked to it using the signs.

_____ **4.** In this paragraph, the word **attended** means
- **A.** worked together
- **B.** took care of
- **C.** kept apart from
- **D.** provided money for

© Steck-Vaughn Company

Name ______________________________ Date ______________

Read the story. Choose the phrase that best completes the sentence.

---

1. Blood is a miracle liquid. It flows to every part of the body. Some blood cells carry food and oxygen to body organs. Other blood cells kill germs and help stop cuts from bleeding. People can die if they lose a lot of blood or if their blood cells get sick. Doctors sometimes give people fresh blood to save their lives.

_____ The story mainly tells

A. how many blood cells are made by the body
B. how important blood is
C. why people can die from loss of blood
D. why sick people are sometimes given blood

---

2. People do not really use music to charm snakes. Snakes have no ears, so they can't hear a flute. The snake charmer startles the snake by waving a hand near it. The snake lifts its head to look around. The charmer then sways back and forth or moves the flute. The snake moves its head to keep an eye on the movement.

_____ The story mainly tells

A. why flute music charms snakes
B. why snakes can't hear sounds
C. how people really charm snakes
D. why snakes have no ears

---

3. A bat can fly at night or even with its eyes closed. But if you cover its ears, it can't fly very well. Bats make sounds that people can't hear. The bats find their way by listening to these sounds as they echo off things. Bats even locate insects to eat by following the sounds that bounce off the bugs. People use their eyes, but bats use their ears to know where they're going.

_____ The story mainly tells

A. how bats use sound
B. what things bats often eat as food
C. how bats fly toward people
D. how people can hear the sounds of bats

Go on to the next page.

© Steck-Vaughn Company

Name ________________________________ Date ________________

4. An old way of collecting worms for fishing is called grunting. To go grunting put a pointed piece of wood into the ground. Then rub a piece of steel back and forth across it. The worms feel the noise in the ground. They come to the surface, and you can just pick them out of the dirt.

_____ The story mainly tells

A. how to run a worm ranch
B. why worms come to the surface
C. how to get worms for fishing bait
D. how to pick worms out of the dirt

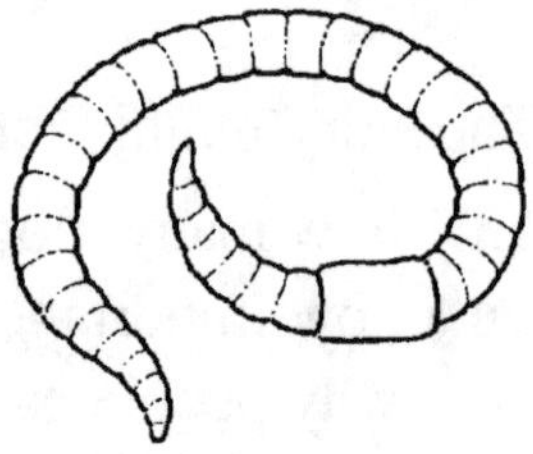

---

5. There could be a treasure in your attic! Did your parents or grandparents save their old toys? Old dolls, train sets, games, and some comic books could be worth a lot of money now. However, just any old toys won't do. Collectors especially want toys that are hard to find and in good condition.

_____ The story mainly tells

A. how to find a treasure in your attic
B. where to get old toys
C. how many different kinds of toys are in the attic
D. which old toys collectors want to buy

---

6. Dolphins are very smart animals. They even have their own language. They talk to each other with clicks, whistles, and grunts. Scientists have been studying this dolphin language. They hope that in the future, people and dolphins will be able to talk to each other.

_____ The story mainly tells

A. how dolphins talk to people
B. how smart dolphins are
C. how dolphins are different from fish
D. which scientists are studying languages

© Steck-Vaughn Company

Name ______________________________ Date ______________

Read the story. Choose the phrase that best completes the sentence.

1. In the 1800s Benjamin Henry Day started the first penny paper. The penny paper was a little newspaper. It cost only one penny. Boys sold it on street corners. The penny paper told stories about interesting people. It also told some stories about how the world was changing. By 1836 the penny paper had become the largest newspaper in the world.

_____ The story mainly tells

- A. who sold stories about people
- B. how the first penny paper started
- C. when people's lives changed
- D. when Benjamin Henry Day was born

2. Deer are the only animals with bones sticking out of their heads. Some animals have horns, but horns aren't bones. They're more like fingernails. Deer have true bones. Every year two new bones grow from the top of a deer's head. At first the bones are soft and covered with skin. Later the skin dries up. The deer rubs off the skin. The bones get hard. The deer uses these horns for fighting.

_____ The story mainly tells

- A. what deer like to use for fighting
- B. how deer grow bones out of their heads
- C. which animals have horns on their heads
- D. why deer have fingernails

3. For years scientists have wanted to know the spider's secret. The threads of spider webs are so tiny, yet so strong. How can these threads be so strong? Now scientists have found out. The inside of the spider's thread is soft. It helps the web stretch without breaking. The outside of the web is hard and strong.

_____ The story mainly tells

- A. who makes thread soft
- B. how spiders make strong thread
- C. how scientists make strong thread
- D. why spiders spin webs

Name ______________________________ Date ______________

Read the story. Choose the phrase that best completes the sentence.

1. Camels have adapted well to the desert. The large humps on their backs hold fat that can serve as food. Camels don't sweat very much, so they don't need much water. The camel's broad feet don't sink in the sand. Long eyelashes and big eyelids protect their eyes from the sun.

_____ The story mainly tells

- A. why camels don't sink in the sand
- B. what the hump of a camel is for
- C. how the camel is suited to live in the desert
- D. why camels do not need a lot of water

2. Bees talk to one another by dancing. When one bee finds flowers for food, it flies back to the hive. The movements it makes tell the bees where the flowers are. If the bee moves in a small circle, the flowers are close. A bee moves slowly in a figure eight when the flowers are over one hundred yards away. Bees may tell about food that is as far as six miles away.

_____ The story mainly tells

- A. how far bees may fly searching for food
- B. how bees talk with each other
- C. what kind of flowering plants bees prefer
- D. how bees collect their food from plants

3. Someday we may mine asteroids for iron, nickel, and even gold. People think that asteroids and meteors may be made of these metals. Most asteroids in our solar system are far away. They float between Mars and Jupiter. It would be very hard to mine them. However, if Earth runs out of some important metals, we may have to try it.

_____ The story mainly tells

- A. where most asteroids are found
- B. what asteroids are made from
- C. when Earth will run out of metals
- D. where metals may be mined in the future

Name ______________________ Date ______________

Read the story. Choose the phrase that best completes the sentence.

---

1. The first hot-air balloon was made by papermakers. They got the idea when they saw ashes rising from a fire. They turned paper bags upside-down over the fire. Just as they had hoped, the bags filled with hot air and floated up. Soon they tried bigger bags made out of paper and then cloth. Finally in 1783 people took their first ride in a hot-air balloon. The age of flight had begun!

_____ The story mainly tells

A. how the hot-air balloon was invented
B. how paper bags floated up
C. why ashes rise over a hot fire
D. how hot-air balloons are made

---

2. The funny bone got its name as the result of a funny mix-up. There is a bone that goes from your shoulder to your elbow. The scientific name for this bone is *humerus*. If you drop the *e* and add two *o's*, the word becomes *humorous,* which means funny. Somehow someone got the two words confused.

_____ The story mainly tells

A. which bone is found in your arm
B. how the funny bone got its name
C. why the bone hurts when you bump it
D. where a nerve runs

---

3. How old is old? Some insects live only a few hours. But some sea turtles live for hundreds of years. What if an insect and a turtle were born at the same instant? The insect would be old after an hour, but the turtle would still be just a baby. A person born at the same time would be old when the turtle was middle-aged.

_____ The story mainly tells

A. how the meaning of *old* depends on the creature
B. how long turtles live before they are old
C. which insects live a few hours
D. how long people live

© Steck-Vaughn Company

Name ______________________________ Date ______________

Read the story. Choose the phrase that best completes the sentence.

1. If gum ever sticks on your clothes, don't try to wash them. Otherwise the gum may never come off. Put an ice cube on the gum. That will harden it so you can try to scrape it off with a table knife. Try nail polish remover. It can sometimes melt gum. If the gum is from a burst bubble, try chewing more gum and using it to lift off the stuck pieces.

_____ The story mainly tells

A. how chewing gum was invented
B. how to melt gum
C. how to use nail polish remover
D. how to remove gum from your clothes

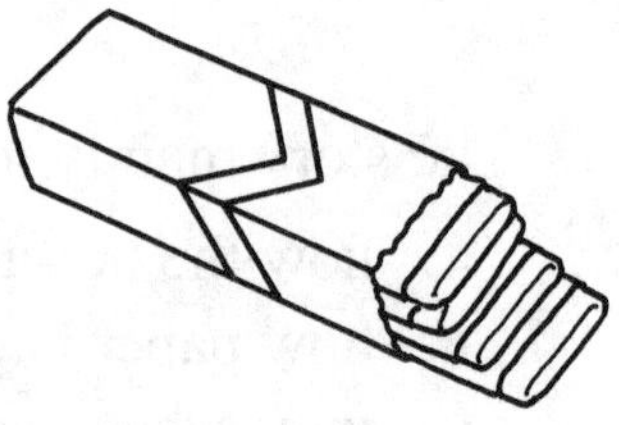

2. Scientists have been studying how people talk to each other. In one study the scientists asked people about their feelings. Do people talk more about sad and angry feelings? Or do they talk more about happy and proud feelings? Scientists found out that people talk about unhappy feelings twice as much as happy ones.

_____ The story mainly tells

A. how to get over sad and angry feelings
B. what scientists have learned about feelings
C. which feelings people talk about most often
D. how often people brag about feeling unhappy

3. Most teenagers think their bodies have problems. Most girls think they are too fat. Eight out of 10 girls go on diets before they are 18. Most teenage boys think they are too thin. They try to build up more muscles. Even if teenagers don't exactly think they are ugly, they would still like to make improvements. It takes teenagers a while to learn that their bodies are really all right the way they are.

_____ The story mainly tells

A. how girls can lose weight
B. how teenagers see their bodies
C. how to improve your looks
D. why teenage boys are skinny

© Steck-Vaughn Company

Name ________________________________ Date ______________

Read the story. Choose the phrase that best completes the sentence.

---

1. Garlic was important in the history of Chicago. Jacques Marquette was a French priest. In 1674, bad health forced him to stop his journey for the winter. He stayed where wild garlic grew. Garlic soup and a fire helped keep Marquette warm. In fact, eating the garlic saved him from getting sick. The place where he stayed was called Checagou. Checagou is a Native American word. It means "place of garlic." That place is now named Chicago.

_____ The story mainly tells

A. how Chicago got its name
B. where Chicago is
C. how to make garlic soup
D. about winter in Checagou

---

2. The gecko, a small lizard, can do something special. It can shed its tail when attacked. When it drops off, the tail wriggles on the ground. The wriggling tail may confuse an attacker. This gives the gecko time to escape. New cells will grow where the tail has dropped off. This growth is called a bud. The bud grows into a new tail. After 8 to 12 months, the gecko has a full-sized tail.

_____ The story mainly tells

A. what a bud is
B. how a gecko gets away from its attacker
C. what a gecko is
D. about a gecko's unusual tail

---

3. Marian Anderson was a famous opera singer. She wanted to sing in Washington, D.C. The owners of a concert hall turned her away. They would not let her sing there because she was African American. The president's wife heard about this. She was very angry. She let Marian sing on the steps of the Lincoln Memorial. On Easter, 1939, Marian Anderson sang in Washington. More than 75,000 people came to hear her.

_____ The story mainly tells about

A. Marian Anderson's concert in Washington
B. Marian Anderson's music
C. Marian Anderson's visit to the Lincoln Memorial
D. Marian Anderson's friendship with a president

© Steck-Vaughn Company

Name ______________________________ Date ______________

Read the story. Choose the phrase that best completes the sentence.

---

1. The moon has one-sixth the gravity of Earth. Everything weighs six times less on the moon. One woman weighs 120 pounds on Earth. But on the moon, she would weigh only 20 pounds. She could jump higher on the moon than she could on Earth. A blue whale weighs 150 tons. If a blue whale could go to the moon, it would weigh just 25 tons.

_____ The story mainly tells

A. how to get to the moon
B. about weight differences on Earth and the moon
C. what a woman weighs on the moon
D. how much a blue whale weighs

---

2. Thurgood Marshall believed in equal rights under the law. For many years he worked as a lawyer for the National Association for the Advancement of Colored People. He won many Supreme Court cases. In 1967 he became the first African American on the Supreme Court. Judge Marshall spent his life fighting for the rights of all Americans.

_____ The story mainly tells

A. that Marshall became a lawyer
B. about a man who believed in equal rights
C. about the National Association for the Advancement of Colored People
D. about how to become a Supreme Court justice

---

3. John Walker was a British chemist and inventor. He was trying to invent an explosive material for guns. Walker mixed some chemicals with a stick. Then he scraped the stick on the floor to remove the chemicals. As he scraped the stick, it burst into flames. This gave Walker the idea of making matches. Walker's matches were first sold in 1827.

_____ The story mainly tells

A. how matches were invented
B. what chemicals are used to make matches
C. about match safety
D. about chemical safety

© Steck-Vaughn Company

Name ______________________________ Date ______________

Read the story. Choose the phrase that best completes the sentence.

1. Thousands of years ago, someone was traveling across the desert. For food he carried sheep's milk in a goatskin bag. But the hot desert sun turned the milk thick and sour. He was hungry, so he ate the strange stuff. To his surprise he liked it! That's how yogurt was discovered.

_____ The story mainly tells

- **A.** which foods to take in the desert
- **B.** how yogurt tastes
- **C.** how yogurt was first made
- **D.** how to survive in the desert

2. If you like surfing, sailing, or other water sports, watch out! You could get *surfer's ear.* With this problem you become hard of hearing or even deaf. The cold water and wind make your ear grow shut. It's easy to prevent the problem. Just wear ear plugs.

_____ The story mainly tells

- **A.** how water sports can cause an ear problem
- **B.** how your ears can change shape
- **C.** how you can close your ears
- **D.** what cold-weather surfing is like

3. Electronic watches don't have springs and gears. Instead they have small batteries, tiny pieces of quartz, and special computers. Of course, the computers are not the kind you can use to play a video game. They only measure how electricity moves through the quartz.

_____ The story mainly tells

- **A.** how different computers measure electricity
- **B.** how an electronic watch works
- **C.** how computers help write reports
- **D.** how to lose a minute a year

© Steck-Vaughn Company

Name ______________________________ Date ______________

Read the story. Choose the phrase that best completes the sentence.

1. When baseball was new, players had to throw the ball and hit the runner to make an out. The ball had to be big and soft so the runners wouldn't be hurt. Later someone invented the tag out to make the game more exciting. That caused some other big changes. The ball could be smaller and harder. The smaller ball could be thrown faster, and batters could hit it farther. Thus the modern game of baseball was born.

_____ The story mainly tells

A. how baseball changed
B. how people used to make an out in baseball
C. how large old baseballs were
D. how far a modern baseball can be hit

2. If your last name is Chang, then you are one of at least one hundred million people in the world with that name! If your name is Smith, then you belong to a group of over two million people in the United States alone. People in some countries have last names with only one letter. In Korea the name *O* is the most popular one-letter name. In Burma the name *E* means *calm.*

_____ The story mainly tells

A. what it's like to have an unusual name
B. how common some last names are
C. which names are common in Korea and Burma
D. how many people are named Smith

3. The early settlers found gold in many parts of the country. Not many of them would take the time to look for it because there was just a small amount. Then in 1848 someone found plenty of gold. It was in California. The next year thousands of prospectors started the Gold Rush. They were called the forty-niners. They panned for gold in the gravel in rivers. Some got very rich, but others weren't so lucky.

_____ The story mainly tells

A. how to pan for gold in rivers
B. how the California Gold Rush happened
C. which people were called the forty-niners
D. what gold is like

© Steck-Vaughn Company

Name ______________________________ Date ______________

Read the story. Choose the phrase that best completes the sentence.

1. The hamburger came from Hamburg, Germany. The first hamburger was just raw ground beef. When the Germans first came to America, they brought the idea with them. But other people did not like raw meat. They decided to cook it. The first cooked hamburger on a bun was served in 1904.

_____ The story mainly tells

A. where hamburgers were first made
B. what the first hamburger was made of
C. how hamburgers came to be
D. how raw ground beef is used

2. Norman Zellers was a regular 13-year-old kid who lived in Illinois. One day he decided to climb the tree in his front yard. Norman sat in the tree for two months! His mother brought him food and fresh clothes. Finally Norman came down to earth. Why did he want to sit in a tree for two months? "Just because it was there!" he said.

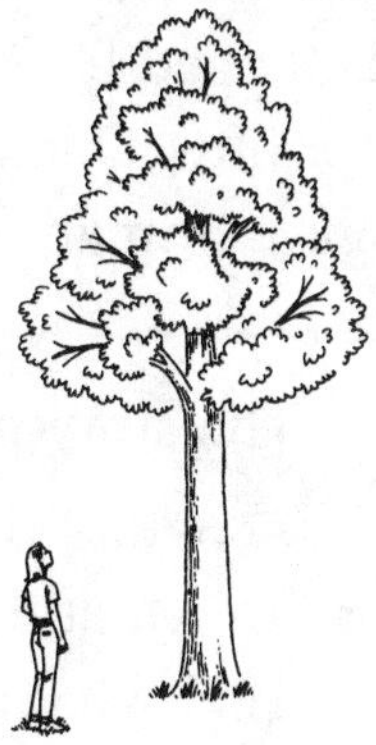

_____ The story mainly tells

A. which things people do to set records
B. what Norman Zellers did for two months
C. what Norman's mother did
D. why Norman climbed the tree

3. A statue called *Motherland* serves as the Russian Statue of Liberty. It is a woman with her arms spread wide. She is holding a sword in one hand. It looks as if she is leading an army into battle. *Motherland* was built in honor of the Russian victory against the Germans during World War II.

_____ The story mainly tells

A. how a woman leads armies into battle
B. what the Russian Statue of Liberty is like
C. how the Russians beat the Germans in the war
D. why the tallest statue in the world holds a sword

Name ______________________ Date ____________

Read the story. Choose the phrase that best completes the sentence.

1. Some sounds are too high for humans to hear. These are called ultrasonic sounds. Bats make these sounds. The sounds help them fly through the dark. Engineers use ultrasonic sounds, too. The sounds help them find flaws inside of objects. Doctors look at babies before they are born, using ultrasonic equipment.

_____ The story mainly tells

A. about how bats find their way through the dark
B. what engineers do
C. about the many ways that ultrasonic sounds are used
D. about ways that doctors use ultrasonic sound

2. Ludwig van Beethoven was deaf in his later years. One of the last pieces of music he wrote was the *Ninth Choral Symphony*. It was performed by solo singers, a chorus, and an orchestra. He sat with the musicians while they played. When they finished, the crowd stood and clapped for Beethoven. But he was deaf. He did not know that they were clapping for him. One of the singers pulled on his sleeve. Surprised, he stood as the audience gave him an ovation.

_____ The story mainly tells

A. that Beethoven was a talented, well-loved composer
B. that the musicians applauded Beethoven
C. what a singer did to Beethoven
D. why Beethoven wrote the *Ninth Choral Symphony*

3. The highest mountain is not Mount Everest. In fact, it is not found on Earth. It is on Mars. Olympus Mons is about 95,000 feet high. That is over three times as high as Mount Everest.

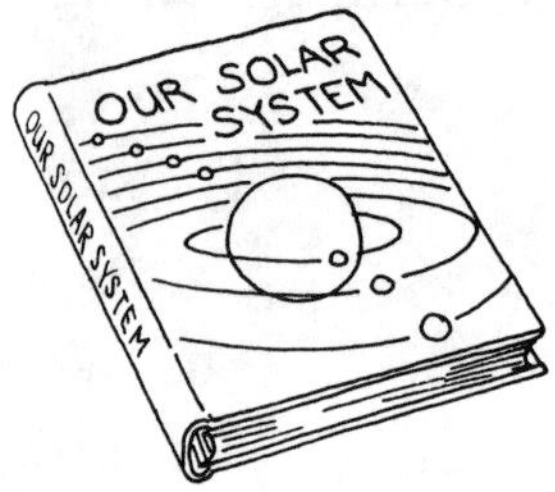

_____ The story mainly tells

A. where Olympus Mons is located
B. where Mount Everest is located
C. how high Mount Everest is
D. that Olympus Mons is the highest mountain known

Name ______________________________ Date ______________

Read the story. Choose the phrase that best completes the sentence.

1. In March 1907 Robert Peary and Matthew Henson set out for the North Pole. They had made many trips together. Henson, an African American, spoke the Innuit language. He built sleds and trained teams of dogs. The two men had twice tried to reach the North Pole. Each time cold weather stopped them. On April 6 they were a few miles from the North Pole. Peary was ill. Matthew Henson went on. Henson placed the first United States flag at the North Pole.

_____ The story mainly tells

- A. about the first American to reach the North Pole
- B. about weather at the North Pole
- C. about the Innuit language
- D. about Peary and Henson's friendship

2. *Love* is a special term used for keeping score in tennis. Love is the English version of the French word *l'oeuf.* L'oeuf means *egg*. In tennis l'oeuf means *nothing"* because 0 is shaped like an egg. When the tennis score is love–forty, think egg–forty!

_____ The story mainly tells

- A. what a French egg is
- B. what *love* means in tennis
- C. how to keep score in tennis
- D. what *l'oeuf* means

3. More than one hundred thousand hairs grow on a person's head. Each hair grows out of a tiny hole in the skin. This hole is called a follicle. The shape of the follicle makes the hair straight, wavy, or curly. Round follicles make straight hair. An oval follicle makes wavy hair. A square follicle makes hair that is curly.

_____ The story mainly tells

- A. what hair is made of
- B. about curly hair
- C. why people have straight hair
- D. what a hair follicle does

© Steck-Vaughn Company

Name ______________________________ Date ______________

Read the story. Choose the phrase that best completes the sentence.

1. The most dangerous part of a space flight comes at the end. When a spacecraft comes back from space, it moves very fast. As it enters Earth's atmosphere, it heats up. But the craft has a heat shield. It keeps the craft cool and protects the astronauts. The craft must enter the atmosphere with the heat shield facing forward. Otherwise, the craft could burn up.

_____ The story mainly tells

A. that an astronaut stays warm
B. about the way a heat shield protects a spacecraft
C. about the way a craft enters the atmosphere
D. about the safest part of a space flight

2. Francis Scott Key fought in the War of 1812. He was taken prisoner by the British. They held him on a small ship. One night he watched a battle from the ship. He saw the American flag flying over Fort Henry. He watched rockets and bombs light up the sky. The next morning he saw that the flag was still there. The United States had won the battle. He wrote a poem about what he saw. The words of his poem became the song *The Star-Spangled Banner.*

_____ The story mainly tells

A. about the history of *The Star-Spangled Banner*
B. about the War of 1812
C. who won the battle of Fort Henry
D. about life as a British prisoner of war

3. Two brothers in France showed the first film in a movie theater. They were Auguste and Louis Lumiere. They made a film of workers leaving a factory. They showed it in Paris in 1895. They made another film about a train. It was so good that people ran away from the screen. They thought the train was real.

_____ The story mainly tells

A. about films that scared people
B. about films made in France
C. who invented the first film
D. about the films of the Lumiere brothers

© Steck-Vaughn Company

Name ______________________________ Date ______________

Read the story. Choose the phrase that best completes the sentence.

1. Ruth was cutting up vegetables for supper. "Ouch!" she screamed. She had cut her finger to the bone. Grace hurried into the room. "Lie down before you pass out," she said. "Press down hard on the cut with a clean cloth." Later a doctor sewed up the cut. The cut healed after two weeks.

_____ From this story you can tell that

A. Grace was Ruth's mother
B. Grace knew first aid
C. Ruth passed out three times
D. Ruth likes to cook

2. Serious dancers begin their training when they're very young. By the age of three, these dancers have already begun to learn a few dance steps. Dancers spend years learning how to move smoothly. They practice for hours each day. Still, young dancers must go to school like other children. The only time they can practice dance is after school.

_____ From this story you can tell that

A. most dancers never learn spelling
B. learning how to dance is a secret
C. dancers have to work very hard
D. three-year-olds are the best dancers

3. The last months of the year are named September, October, November, and December. These names come from Latin words. The words mean *seventh, eighth, ninth,* and *tenth.* But today September is the ninth month. Also, December is the twelfth month. Why? Long ago the Romans had a calendar with ten months. They noticed that they didn't have enough months to fill a year. So they added more months.

November

Sun	Mon	Tues	Wed	Thur	Fri	Sat
			1	2	3	4
5	6	7	8	9	10	11
12	13	14	15	16	17	18
19	20	21	22	23	24	25
26	27	28	29	30		

_____ From this story you can tell that

A. December is now the ninth month
B. the calendar has never changed
C. long ago November came right after September
D. the Romans probably added two more months

Go on to the next page.

Name ______________________________ Date ______________

4. Farmers have known for a long time that pigs like toys. Research shows that when pigs play with toys, they are less likely to harm one another. What kind of toys do pigs like? Reports say that pigs are fond of rubber hoses. They like to shake them and chew on the ends.

_____ You can tell that

- A. toys help improve the way pigs behave
- B. pigs are good playmates
- C. farmers play with pigs
- D. pigs do not share their toys

---

5. One of the oldest games in the world is hockey. The ancient Greeks and Persians played it. So did Native Americans. The name comes from an old French word, *hoquet.* It is the word for a shepherd's crooked staff, or stick.

_____ From this story you can tell that

- A. hockey is played with a ball
- B. the French have played hockey for a long time
- C. hockey is now played by shepherds
- D. hockey will not last much longer

---

6. Will Rogers was a famous cowboy with a sense of humor. He was a writer and a star of the stage, movies, and radio. Many statues honor him, and many places are named for him. Near Dodge City, Kansas, there is a wheat field shaped like him. Different grains form the features of his face. You can see this Will Rogers wheat field from an airplane.

_____ You can tell that

- A. Will Rogers was a farmer
- B. Will Rogers thought wheat fields were funny places
- C. the Will Rogers wheat field is very small
- D. the wheat field face is hard to see from the ground

© Steck-Vaughn Company

Name ______________________________ Date ______________

Read the story. Choose the phrase that best completes the sentence.

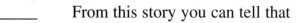

1. Spaceships can go seven miles a second. That sounds fast, but it's really slow. A trip to Mars takes a spaceship about nine months. Light is much faster. It travels about two hundred thousand miles a second. Light travels faster than anything else. If people could ride on a ray of light, a trip to Mars would take five minutes.

_____ From this story you can tell that

A. spaceships can now move as fast as light
B. long space trips will need very fast spaceships
C. a trip around Earth would take five minutes
D. traveling in space is dangerous

2. Once dodo birds lived on an island. They ate the seeds of one kind of tree. The seeds had hard shells. But dodo birds had strong stomachs. Their stomach juices broke up the shells. Because of this, the seeds could grow. The last dodo birds died out years ago. Scientists found that the trees were dying out, too. They wanted to save the trees. So they decided to feed the hard seeds to turkeys. Turkeys have strong stomachs. With their help the trees live on.

_____ From this story you can tell that

A. animals ate all the dodo birds years ago
B. the seeds were the dodo's only food
C. the tree couldn't grow without a bird's help
D. birds can't eat seeds with hard shells

3. There weren't always oranges in Europe. People from the Far East brought oranges to Europe during the Middle Ages. Later, sailors from Europe brought oranges to America. Now the United States grows a million tons of oranges each year.

_____ From this story you can tell that

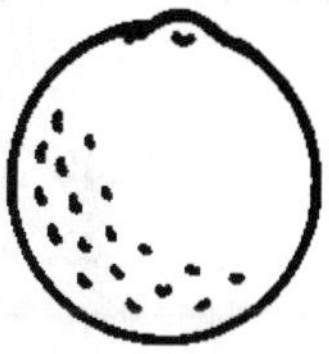

A. the first oranges probably grew in the Far East
B. orange trees make fruit only in winter
C. orange trees have blue flowers
D. there were many wars during the Middle Ages

© Steck-Vaughn Company

Name ______________________________ Date ______________

Read the story. Choose the phrase that best completes the sentence.

1. Many people in the United States are sports fans. They like sports. Football is the sport most people like. The second most popular sport is baseball. The third favorite sport is fishing. There is one interesting thing about fishing. Fishing fans actually fish.

_____ From this story you can tell that most Americans

- A. play baseball and football
- B. watch fishing contests
- C. watch football or baseball games
- D. eat fish

2. Tugboats help link the city of Seattle to the sea. The small, strong tugs guide large ships into and out of the harbor. Without the tugs the big ships could not make the trip safely. To honor the tugs, Seattle holds tugboat races each spring. At that time the harbor is full of stubby boats splashing in the water like playful whales.

_____ You can tell that tugs are

- A. used only in the spring
- B. unsafe
- C. hard to steer
- D. necessary

3. William H. Harrison was the ninth president of the United States. He was sworn in as president in 1841. At the event he gave a long speech. In fact, his speech was the longest ever made by a new president. At his speech, the weather was very cold. Harrison grew ill and died 31 days later. He is now known as the president who gave the longest speech. He is also known as the one who served the shortest term.

_____ The story suggests that William Harrison

- A. was president only a short while
- B. liked cold weather
- C. liked short speeches
- D. was a funny president

© Steck-Vaughn Company

Name ____________________ Date ____________

Read the story. Choose the phrase that best completes the sentence.

1. The wedding ring is a sign of love. Long ago people thought that a wedding ring should be worn on the fourth finger of the left hand. Then the ring would be on the same side of the body as the heart. People also believed that a vein ran from the fourth finger straight to the heart.

_____ Today people wear wedding rings on their left hand because

- A. they want to protect their hearts
- B. it is a custom from days gone by
- C. the ring fits best on the fourth finger
- D. they need a sign of love

2. Today a book is a stack of printed papers bound in a cover. Today's books are easy to carry. But years ago books were different. Each book was made of heavy clay tablets with carvings on them. The tablets of one book filled a long shelf. It would have taken many trips to carry such a book from the shelf to a reading table.

_____ One clay tablet can best be compared to

- A. a page in a modern book
- B. a carving in a museum
- C. the cover of a book
- D. part of a library shelf

3. Rice is one of the most important crops in the world. Over half the people on Earth depend on rice as their main source of food. Most of the world's rice is grown in Asia. People there do not take the husk, or covering, off the grains of rice. When rice is eaten that way, it is especially healthful. Most of the vitamins in rice are found in the husk.

_____ When the husk is taken off,

- A. the rice loses vitamins
- B. people in Asia will not eat it
- C. the rice does not taste as good
- D. it can be sold in other countries

© Steck-Vaughn Company

Name ______________________________ Date ______________

Read the story. Choose the phrase that best completes the sentence.

1. What drink do we like on a hot day? Lots of people drink lemonade. This sweet and sour drink cools us off. Children set up stands to sell it. Families take it on picnics. Neighbors sip it on porches. Lemonade is popular in America. It was first made in Paris, France, in 1630.

_____ From the story you can tell that

A. most lemonade comes from Paris, France
B. more lemonade is sold in summer than in winter
C. lemonade is heated before it is served
D. lemonade is a healthy drink

2. Ranchers in Texas had a problem. Coyotes and other wild animals were killing their sheep and goats. So some ranchers began using donkeys to protect the herds. The donkeys do a good job. The coyotes are terrified of the teeth and sharp hooves of the donkeys.

_____ You can tell that when donkeys see coyotes they

A. kick and bite
B. tell the ranchers
C. run away
D. hide the herds

3. A man named Theodor Geisel once wrote a book about a street from his childhood. It was called *And to Think That I Saw It on Mulberry Street.* Fifty years later the author returned to Mulberry Street in Springfield, Massachusetts. What did he see? He saw people dressed up like the funny-looking creatures in his books. The author was called Dr. Seuss, and most of the creatures wanted his autograph.

_____ You can tell that

A. Dr. Seuss traveled around the world
B. Dr. Seuss still lives on Mulberry Street
C. Dr. Seuss received a warm welcome in Springfield
D. the creatures were people dressed like Dr. Seuss

© Steck-Vaughn Company

Name ______________________________ Date ______________

Read the story. Choose the phrase that best completes the sentence.

1. Grace opened her eyes. "What time is it?" she wondered. The room was very dark until she drew back the curtains. A mockingbird began its song, and from another room she smelled burning toast. "My roommate will never learn to set the toaster right," she thought.

_____ From this story you can tell that Grace

A. has awakened from a midday nap
B. has fallen asleep at school
C. is waking up in the morning
D. is going to bed at night

2. Jimmy asked Jeanine to help him glue on his false mustache. She asked him if her gray wig was crooked. They looked across the floor at the old-fashioned furniture lit by the spotlights. When they saw the huge curtain begin to rise and heard the applause, they wished each other luck.

_____ From this story you can tell that

A. Jimmy and Jeanine are opening an antique store
B. Jimmy and Jeanine are watching a movie
C. Jimmy and Jeanine are about to act in a play
D. Jimmy and Jeanine are brother and sister

3. The man wriggled his toes in the sand and then returned to the towel on the ground. He picked up the pair of binoculars by the towel and looked through them. The ship in the distance didn't have an American flag. But he couldn't tell what country's flag the ship was flying.

_____ You can tell that the man

A. is a spy for a foreign country
B. is standing on a beach looking out in the ocean
C. doesn't have very much money
D. is camping in the mountains during the winter

© Steck-Vaughn Company

Name ______________________________ Date ______________

Read the story. Choose the phrase that best completes the sentence.

1. Many Americans like to eat Chinese food. At the end of the meal, fortune cookies are served. These folded-up cookies have messages in them. Some messages tell what the future will bring. Other messages give advice. Still others are just wise sayings. All messages are written for Americans. Fortune cookies are never served in China.

_____ From this story you can tell that

A. the messages are in Chinese
B. people in China can't read
C. fortune cookies are an American custom
D. people in China don't like cookies

2. What causes the traffic light to change colors? A timer in a box near the light is set for a certain number of seconds. But the number of seconds isn't the same all the time. At night when there's less traffic, the light may change more slowly.

_____ You can tell that during rush hour

A. the light stays red all the time
B. the lights change more quickly
C. the timer always breaks
D. the light stays yellow

3. What if the sun were the size of a grapefruit? Then Earth would be the size of the head of a pin. Earth would be about half a football field away from the sun. Jupiter would be the size of a marble. It would be about one and one-half football fields away from the sun. Uranus would be the size of a pea five football fields away from the sun.

_____ You can tell that

A. Earth is bigger than Jupiter
B. it might be very hot on Uranus
C. Earth is smaller than Uranus
D. you can throw a football from Earth to Jupiter

© Steck-Vaughn Company

Name ______________________________ Date ______________

Read the story. Choose the phrase that best completes the sentence.

---

1. Miniature horses are becoming very popular. They look like a horse but are only as big as a German Shepherd dog. These little horses come in many colors. They can learn tricks and earn ribbons at horse shows. Best of all, they eat much less than regular horses.

_____ You can tell that the little horses

A. can pull big loads
B. are fast compared to normal horses
C. can only be brown
D. cannot be ridden by an adult

---

2. For a long time, the size of the universe was a mystery. Astronomers did not know how big it was. Most thought our Milky Way galaxy made up the whole universe. In the 1920s Edwin Hubble proved them wrong. He found galaxies beyond our own. Hubble gained fame for his work. The Hubble space telescope was named for him.

_____ From this story you can tell that

A. the universe is not very big
B. Hubble discovered a telescope in space
C. the Milky Way makes up the whole universe
D. Hubble helped show the real size of the universe

---

3. The sun and robots are spoken of as "he." A ship is called "she." Hurricanes used to be given women's names, but that practice was changed after people complained. People object to identifying some things with women and others with men.

_____ You can tell that

A. *Sun* is a name for a man
B. tornadoes are given women's names
C. hurricanes are no longer named only for women
D. ships are like women

© Steck-Vaughn Company

Name ____________________________ Date ______________

Read the story. Choose the phrase that best completes the sentence.

1. People who sew use patterns. But before 1863 patterns were hard to use. Up to fifteen patterns were printed on one page. All patterns were the same size. Then the Butterick family decided to make patterns in different sizes. They put their easy-to-use patterns in separate envelopes.

_____ You can tell that

A. after 1863 fewer people made clothes
B. clothes were easier to make after 1863
C. clothes were made of better materials after 1863
D. people didn't know how to sew before 1863

2. Actors think many things are bad luck. They don't whistle in the dressing room. They don't like to use peacock feathers, umbrellas, and real mirrors on stage. They feel that using the color green on stage is also unlucky. And no one ever says "good luck" to an actor. Instead, people say "break a leg."

_____ You can tell that actors almost never

A. sing in the dressing room
B. eat dinner at restaurants
C. look at themselves in the mirror
D. use a green rug on stage

3. Namiko Mori designs clothes for customers who have disabilities. She makes raincoats that fit over wheelchairs. She also makes shirts with elastic buttonholes so the shirts are easy to button. Pants are made larger so people can put them on with less trouble. The name of Mori's shop is Helpers.

_____ You can tell that

A. Namiko Mori has a disability
B. Mori's store sells mostly dresses
C. Mori's customers have special needs
D. wheelchairs wear clothes

© Steck-Vaughn Company

Name ______________________________ Date ______________

Read the story. Choose the phrase that best completes the sentence.

---

1. The woman waited while the child stood at the glass counter. The boy walked slowly from one end of the counter to the other. His mother tapped her foot more and more impatiently. Behind the counter a man waited with a scoop in his hand. Finally the boy spoke. “Vanilla,” he said.

_____ You can tell that this story takes place in

A. a gas station
B. a clothing store
C. an ice cream store
D. a doctor’s office

---

2. He heard the steady drumming sound he made on the pavement. One foot was becoming sore, but he didn’t let himself feel the pain. At last he passed the park bench with the broken seat. “One more mile to go,” he thought.

_____ From this you can tell that the man

A. is running in a gym
B. is running along a route he often takes
C. is a stranger to the neighborhood
D. has broken his foot

---

3. William went inside the small wire fence and knelt down. He gently took a leaf in his fingers. He closely examined the little pattern of holes along one edge. “The rabbits have raided us again,” he said to his wife. Then he snapped off the one remaining head of lettuce and stood up.

_____ From this story you can tell that the man and his wife

A. run a farm for their living
B. are raising rabbits for pets
C. are buying food at a grocery store
D. have a small vegetable garden

© Steck-Vaughn Company

Name ______________________ Date ______________

Read the story. Choose the phrase that best completes the sentence.

1. Bob Siekman of Pyote, Texas, has an unusual hobby. He collects old fire trucks. As a youth, Bob watched a man build a fire truck. Young Bob thought fires were very exciting. As a man, Bob continued his interest in fire trucks by collecting them. He now has five old fire trucks in his collection.

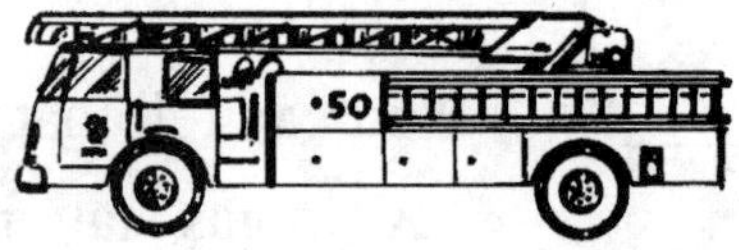

_____ The story does not tell

A. where Bob Siekman lives
B. about Bob Siekman's hobby
C. how many old fire trucks Bob Siekman owns
D. where Bob Siekman finds the old fire trucks

2. In 1916 a great fire swept through north Ontario. It left behind a thousand square miles of burned forests and farmland. Six Canadian towns were burned, too. William Dowson watched the fire as it neared. Seeing its fury, he feared for his life. He lay face down in a potato patch as the fire roared around him. The smoke and heat were awful, but Dowson survived the fire unharmed.

_____ The story suggests that William Dowson

A. thought quickly in an emergency
B. was a news reporter
C. liked to eat potatoes
D. was not afraid of the fire

3. One night in 1816, Mary Shelley and some friends gathered. They took turns telling scary stories. At last Mary's turn came. She told a story of a doctor. The doctor tried to create a man but built a monster instead. Two years later Mary published the story in a book called *Frankenstein*.

_____ The story does not tell

A. when Mary Shelley and her friends gathered
B. when Mary Shelley's book was published
C. what the other scary stories were about
D. what Mary Shelley's scary story was about

Name ____________________ Date ____________

Read the story. Choose the phrase that best completes the sentence.

---

1. Alfred Wegener looked at a world map. He noticed a strange thing. All the continents looked like jigsaw pieces. All the pieces seemed to fit together. Wegener thought about this idea for a long time. In 1912 he offered a new theory. He claimed that all the continents were once a large landmass. Then over time the continents moved apart. Wegener called his theory continental drift. But other scientists did not accept his ideas until 40 years later.

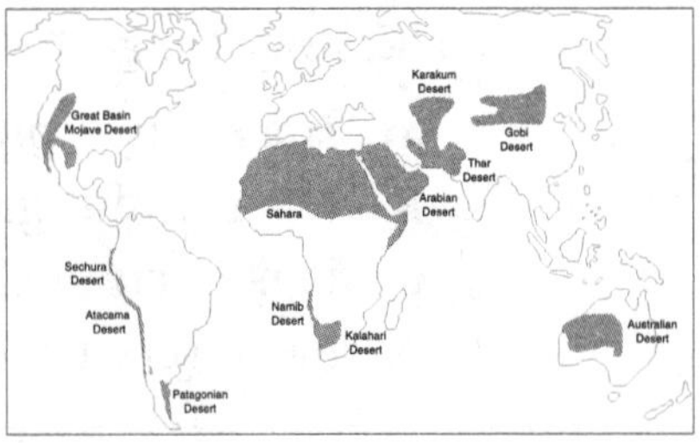

_____ The story suggests that Wegener's theory

- **A.** was about jigsaw puzzles
- **B.** was accepted immediately
- **C.** did not have a name
- **D.** explained how the continents were formed

---

2. At the age of three, Louis Braille lost his sight. But he did not let this loss stand in his way. As a teenager he became an accomplished musician. At age 19 Braille began teaching the blind in Paris. One year later, in 1829, he developed a system of printing for those who had lost their sight. The Braille system uses 63 sets of 6 raised dots. This system, often called Braille, is still in use today.

_____ The story does not tell

- **A.** what Louis Braille did as a teenager
- **B.** when Louis Braille became a teacher
- **C.** how Louis Braille lost his sight
- **D.** if the Braille system is still in use

---

3. One common superstition is the fear of the number 13. The fear of 13 shows up in many places. On most airplanes there is no thirteenth row of seats. Most tall buildings do not have a thirteenth floor. And many people feel a bit nervous on Friday the thirteenth.

_____ From this story you cannot tell

- **A.** that the fear of 13 is very common
- **B.** why people fear the number 13
- **C.** if airplanes use 13 as a row number
- **D.** on what day Friday the thirteenth falls

© Steck-Vaughn Company

Name ______________________________ Date ______________

Read the story. Choose the phrase that best completes the sentence.

1. If you look under your kitchen sink, you will see some drain pipes. One pipe is U-shaped. It is called a trap. Harmful gases develop in a sewer line. The curved part of the trap holds a small amount of water. The water closes off the pipe. The trap keeps you safe. The gases can't enter your house and harm you.

_____ The story suggests that the trap

- A. is a straight pipe
- B. lets harmful gases enter your house
- C. is not part of the drain pipe
- D. has a very useful purpose

2. Today many people shake hands when they meet. But the handshake was not always a sign of friendship. Long ago when a man met a stranger, he would reach for his knife. The stranger would do the same. Then the men would slowly circle each other. Certain that no danger was present, they would shake with their weapon hands. The handshake served as a sign of goodwill.

_____ The story suggests that the handshake was

- A. once used by the police
- B. not always a friendly action
- C. part of a funny dance
- D. not a sign of goodwill

3. James Beckwourth was born to a slave mother in 1798. At age 19 James decided to become a scout. He headed to the western United States. He soon became famous as a trapper and mountain man. As a scout he found an important trail through the Sierra Nevada Mountains. This passage was named Beckwourth Pass in honor of him.

_____ The story does not tell

- A. what Beckwourth did for a living
- B. where Beckwourth found an important trail
- C. why Beckwourth was famous
- D. why Beckwourth decided to become a scout

© Steck-Vaughn Company

Name ______________________________ Date ______________

Read the story. Mark whether each statement is an inference or a fact.

---

1. Trees need special care. They must be planted in a certain way. The roots need a lot of room in order to grow. The hole for the roots must be very wide and deep. The roots grow deep into the earth. And they spread as wide under the ground as the branches do above the ground.

Fact Inference

- ○ ○ A. Tree roots grow underground.
- ○ ○ B. A large tree needs a big hole.
- ○ ○ C. A tree's roots spread as wide as its branches.
- ○ ○ D. Trees must be planted in a special way.

---

2. It was spring and time to get the garden ready for planting. Chris had a load of dirt delivered to his back yard. For two whole days, Chris shoveled dirt into a wheelbarrow. He put the dirt in the garden. He went back and forth between the dirt pile and the garden. It took many hours and much hard work. On the third day, he saw his neighbor coming over with a wheelbarrow.

Fact Inference

- ○ ○ A. Chris needed another wheelbarrow.
- ○ ○ B. Chris hoped his neighbor would help.
- ○ ○ C. Chris put the dirt in the garden.
- ○ ○ D. Chris had the dirt delivered.

---

3. Nel lives on a farm. She raises chickens for a living. Each morning she goes to the henhouse to collect eggs from the nests. Every week a truck comes to pick up the white eggs for a large grocery store chain in the city. Once every two weeks another truck comes to pick up the brown eggs.

Fact Inference

- ○ ○ A. People buy more white eggs than brown.
- ○ ○ B. Nel lives on a farm.
- ○ ○ C. Trucks pick up the eggs.
- ○ ○ D. Nel likes raising chickens.

Go on to the next page.

© Steck-Vaughn Company

Name ______________________________ Date ______________

4. In the spring, many farmers put beehives in their fields of fruit trees. Bees collect pollen from the flowers on the trees. They eat the pollen. And as they fly, they spread pollen from flower to flower. In this way, they help the trees produce fruit.

Fact	Inference	
○	○	**A.** Farmers put beehives in their fields.
○	○	**B.** Bees collect pollen from the flowers.
○	○	**C.** Farmers need bees in order to grow fruit.
○	○	**D.** Bees do not eat all of the pollen.

---

5. Atlases are made up of maps. One kind of atlas is a historical atlas. It has maps that show how groups of people or countries have gained or lost land over the years. Some maps tell about trips that explorers have made to different countries. The maps can show mountains, deserts, rivers, and oceans. The maps also give facts about the products each country makes and trades with other countries. Historical atlases cover events from the past to the present.

Fact	Inference	
○	○	**A.** Maps can help people study history.
○	○	**B.** Some atlases tell about trade.
○	○	**C.** Atlases are made up of maps.
○	○	**D.** Some maps tell about past wars.

---

6. Bill and Sid collect cans. They sell the cans to a recycling center. Lately business has been so good that they have divided their work in half. Bill's area includes a park where teams play baseball every day. Sid collects cans from office buildings and stores.

Fact	Inference	
○	○	**A.** Many people drink canned drinks.
○	○	**B.** Sid's route includes office buildings.
○	○	**C.** Bill and Sid earn more money now than when they started.
○	○	**D.** Bill's route includes a park.

© Steck-Vaughn Company

Name ______________________________ Date ________________

Read the story. Mark whether each statement is an inference or a fact.

1. Pam and Pat tried out for the soccer team. The coach needed only one more player. She needed a good goalie to block the other team's shots. Last year the team lost every game by more than five goals. During tryouts Pam passed the ball well but couldn't block goal shots. As a practice goalie, Pat saved many shots.

Fact	Inference	
○	○	A. The coach picked Pat to be on the team.
○	○	B. A good goalie can help a team win.
○	○	C. Pat and Pam tried out for the soccer team.
○	○	D. Pam could pass the ball well.

2. Frank loved to play tennis, and he was on the tennis court every day. Frank could hit the ball very hard. He was a good player. One day he met his friend Jim for a game of tennis. Jim had just started playing tennis. After the game Frank said, "I will help you with your shots, Jim."

Fact	Inference	
○	○	A. Frank loved to play tennis.
○	○	B. Frank and Jim met for a game of tennis.
○	○	C. Frank won the game.
○	○	D. Jim was not a good tennis player.

3. A radiator keeps the engine of a car cool. Hot water from the engine runs through hoses to the radiator. The radiator has thousands of air openings. Air rushing past the hoses cools the hot water. A fan forces more air into the radiator when the car is stopped or moving slowly.

Fact	Inference	
○	○	A. The engine would overheat without a radiator.
○	○	B. Radiators have openings for air.
○	○	C. The air cools the hot water.
○	○	D. Cars produce much heat.

© Steck-Vaughn Company
Comprehension 5, SV 6187-7

Name ______________________________ Date ______________

Read the story. Mark whether each statement is an inference or a fact.

1. Each year during the last week in April, the old man began his garden. He planted tomatoes during the second week in May. He weeded the garden as the plants grew. By the middle of summer, the tomatoes were ready to sell. Many people bought them. They liked his red, ripe tomatoes. By Labor Day it was time for the old man to pull up all his tomato plants.

Fact	Inference	
○	○	A. The old man worked hard to grow tomatoes.
○	○	B. The tomatoes were not good after Labor Day.
○	○	C. He weeded the garden as the plants grew.
○	○	D. He sold tomatoes for a very short time.

2. Heavy trucks can destroy roads. To protect the roads, states make truck drivers weigh their cargo. They do this on giant scales at weigh stations along the road. The truck drives onto the scale, and its weight is taken. If the truck is too heavy, it is not allowed to drive any farther.

Fact	Inference	
○	○	A. Heavy trucks can hurt roads.
○	○	B. States make drivers weigh their cargo.
○	○	C. Trucks must not be overloaded.
○	○	D. Weigh stations have scales.

3. A large number of preschools have been set up in the last thirty years. This is because more mothers work during the day. Neither parent can stay at home with the children. They need child care. Many people also believe that preschools are good for young children. In a preschool the children can play and learn from each other.

Fact	Inference	
○	○	A. Children can learn from each other.
○	○	B. More mothers work outside the home.
○	○	C. Parents think child care is important.
○	○	D. Many children go to preschools.

© Steck-Vaughn Company

Name ______________________________ Date ______________

Read the story. Mark whether each statement is an inference or a fact.

1. Most people learn to sail on a small boat. While they are learning, they keep the boat in a protected spot, such as a harbor. First they learn the names of all the parts of the boat. Then they learn how to turn and move the boat with or against the wind. They also learn what to do if the boat turns over. Once people know how to sail a small boat, with practice they can sail a boat of almost any size.

Fact	Inference	
○	○	A. People best learn to sail on a small boat.
○	○	B. It is best to learn to sail in a protected spot.
○	○	C. Sailing takes some skill.
○	○	D. Large boats are harder to sail than small boats.

2. Every day Ricky came home from school and went right to his room. He took his homework with him. When it was dinner time, he came out of his room. Ricky's parents thought he was studying. They were proud of how hard their son was working. They were very surprised when Ricky failed three of his classes.

Fact	Inference	
○	○	A. Ricky was not studying in his room.
○	○	B. Ricky's parents were angry with him.
○	○	C. Ricky went to his room each day.
○	○	D. Ricky failed three of his classes.

3. Megan had practiced her part in the play. She knew her lines backwards and forwards. She was very excited about acting in the play. On the day of the play, she woke up with a terrible sore throat. Her throat hurt too much for her to talk.

Fact	Inference	
○	○	A. Megan was excited about the play.
○	○	B. Megan had a sore throat.
○	○	C. Megan had practiced her part.
○	○	D. Megan was not able to act in the play.

© Steck-Vaughn Company

Name ______________________ Date ____________

Read the story. Mark whether each statement is an inference or a fact.

1. The students painted designs. When they were finished, the teacher told them to look at each painting. She wanted them to find the outline of objects in each design. Some students saw flowers and animals in the pictures. Others saw bottles and boxes. But no one found anything in Bill's picture. He had painted it all black.

Fact	Inference	
○	○	A. Bill didn't make a design.
○	○	B. The teacher was angry with Bill.
○	○	C. Students painted designs.
○	○	D. Bill was in an art class.

2. Long ago if ships wanted to get from Spain to China, they had to sail around Africa. The trip took many months. Some people felt that there must be a better way. So they built a canal in northern Africa. The canal was like a river across the land. Ships could then sail on the canal across the top of Africa. They didn't have to go all the way around.

Fact	Inference	
○	○	A. Africa is a large area of land.
○	○	B. Water surrounds Africa.
○	○	C. Ships can sail on a canal.
○	○	D. The canal shortened the trip to China.

3. The Pony Express carried letters from Missouri to California. Riders rode ten miles and changed horses. They could put saddles on new horses in two minutes. Each rider had to change his horse seven times a day. The Pony Express was replaced by the telegraph. The telegraph sent messages over wires.

Fact	Inference	
○	○	A. The Pony Express was slower than the telegraph.
○	○	B. Riders changed horses after ten miles.
○	○	C. It was very tiring to be a Pony Express rider.
○	○	D. Horses were worn out after ten miles.

Name ______________________________ Date ______________

Read the story. Mark whether each statement is an inference or a fact.

1. Biltmore House is the largest house in the world. It has 250 rooms. George Vanderbilt had the house built near Asheville, North Carolina. Vanderbilt was the son of an American family that made a fortune in the railroad business.

Fact	Inference	
○	○	A. Vanderbilt had the house built.
○	○	B. Biltmore House is in North Carolina.
○	○	C. Vanderbilt was rich.
○	○	D. Biltmore House has 250 rooms.

2. Karen wanted to buy a new pair of roller skates. She decided to set up a yard sale to earn the money. Karen's mother helped her. They collected things around the house that they no longer wanted. Karen made signs and posted them around her neighborhood. Then they arranged the things on card tables in their front yard. A lot of buyers came to the yard sale.

Fact	Inference	
○	○	A. Karen liked to skate.
○	○	B. Karen was willing to work for money.
○	○	C. Karen set up a yard sale.
○	○	D. Karen made signs for the yard sale.

3. Mammals are animals that feed their young with milk. Pigs are the mammals that have the most babies. A pig can have as many as 34 babies at a time. A mother pig is called a sow. Baby pigs that are less than 10 weeks old are called piglets.

Fact	Inference	
○	○	A. Pigs feed their young with milk.
○	○	B. Piglets are very small.
○	○	C. Pigs are mammals.
○	○	D. A pig can have up to 34 babies at a time.

© Steck-Vaughn Company

Name ______________________________ Date ______________

Read the story. Mark whether each statement is an inference or a fact.

1. Parkside Hospital was holding a big bike race. Those who entered would help raise money for the hospital. Robin and Gwen decided to enter the five-mile race. As the girls reached the end of the race, Gwen rode her bike over a hole in the road. She fell off and landed on the street. Although Robin was in the lead, she stopped to make sure Gwen was okay.

Fact	Inference	
○	○	A. The race was five miles long.
○	○	B. Robin and Gwen liked to ride bikes.
○	○	C. Gwen fell off her bike.
○	○	D. Robin was a helpful person.

2. Many books and movies have been written about the story of Robin Hood. Robin Hood was a folk hero who robbed the rich and gave what he took to the poor. Robin Hood is said to have lived in Sherwood Forest. He lived with a band of merry men. Many people have tried to prove he was a real person. But so far no one has been able to show that he really lived.

Fact	Inference	
○	○	A. Robin Hood is a popular story.
○	○	B. People admire Robin Hood.
○	○	C. Robin Hood cared about the poor.
○	○	D. No one can prove that Robin Hood really lived.

3. Jake's dad loved to read books about airplanes. One day Jake was at the library. He noticed a new book about airplanes near the check-out desk. "Wait a minute, please," he said to the librarian. He walked over to get the book. "Could you add this to the books I'm checking out?" he asked.

Fact	Inference	
○	○	A. Jake was checking out books.
○	○	B. Jake was at the library.
○	○	C. Jake's dad liked books about airplanes.
○	○	D. Jake wanted to please his father.

© Steck-Vaughn Company

Name ______________________________ Date ______________

Read the story. Mark whether each statement is an inference or a fact.

1. It had been snowing for two hours. Tanya and her mother decided take a walk in the woods. As they walked, everything seemed very still. The ground looked like a field of cotton. Tanya caught a tiny snowflake on the tip of her tongue. She turned and looked at her mother. Fluffy snowflakes dusted her mother's eyelashes.

Fact	Inference	
○	○	**A.** It was winter.
○	○	**B.** Being out in the snow was fun.
○	○	**C.** Tanya caught a snowflake on her tongue.
○	○	**D.** Tanya and her mother were walking.

2. Hot dogs were named by a newspaper cartoonist from Chicago. One day in 1906, cartoonist Tad Dorgan was at a baseball game. A boy came by selling frankfurters. Dorgan drew a picture of the frankfurters. He made them look like small, long dogs on a bun. Under the cartoon he wrote, "Hot dogs."

Fact	Inference	
○	○	**A.** Hot dogs were first called frankfurters.
○	○	**B.** Tad Dorgan was a cartoonist.
○	○	**C.** People liked the new name.
○	○	**D.** Dorgan's cartoon was printed in the newspaper.

3. Marcie loved bananas. She loved banana splits, banana pudding, and banana ice cream. But her favorite way to eat a banana was to simply peel it and eat it. One day she had just enjoyed her favorite food while sitting on the front steps of her house. She left the peel on the steps. An hour later her mother came home. As she climbed the steps to the front door, she noticed the peel. But it was too late.

Fact	Inference	
○	○	**A.** Marcie left the peel on the steps.
○	○	**B.** Marcie's mother slipped on the peel.
○	○	**C.** Marcie loved bananas.
○	○	**D.** Marcie's mother was angry.

© Steck-Vaughn Company

Name ______________________________ Date ______________

Read the story. Mark whether each statement is an inference or a fact.

1. In 1947 African Americans did not play with whites on the same team. But Jackie Robinson and the Brooklyn Dodgers changed all that. That first day Robinson was on the baseball field, some people cheered him. But others hissed and booed. By the time he died in 1972, African Americans had become important players in all sports.

Fact	Inference	
○	○	**A.** At first some people booed Robinson.
○	○	**B.** Robinson died in 1972.
○	○	**C.** The Dodgers wanted Robinson to play.
○	○	**D.** Robinson had great courage.

2. Brad and his friends were walking home from school. The traffic light had just changed. The "Don't Walk" sign was flashing. His friends kept on walking. But Brad decided to obey the signal. A car screeched to a stop to keep from hitting the boys. A police officer who had been watching walked up to the boys.

Fact	Inference	
○	○	**A.** Brad's friends did not obey the signal.
○	○	**B.** The police officer was watching the boys.
○	○	**C.** Brad obeyed the traffic signal.
○	○	**D.** The police officer gave the boys a ticket.

3. Acid rain is a growing problem. When factories burn coal, they give off harmful gases. These gases mix with falling rain and make a weak acid. The acid falls into lakes and streams. It kills fish, plants, and many trees. To solve the problem, factories need to put in special equipment that keeps the harmful gases from escaping into the air.

Fact	Inference	
○	○	**A.** Acid rain is a costly problem to solve.
○	○	**B.** Many factories don't have special equipment.
○	○	**C.** Acid rain kills fish.
○	○	**D.** Plants cannot live in weak acid.

© Steck-Vaughn Company

Name ______________________________ Date ______________

Read the story. Mark whether each statement is an inference or a fact.

1. A huge fire raced through Chicago in 1871. The story goes that a cow in the O'Leary barn kicked over a lantern. Then the hay caught fire, and the flames spread. This story was made up by a news reporter. But the fire was real. It burned for nearly thirty hours. Its flames destroyed more than seventeen thousand buildings.

Fact	Inference	
○	○	A. The Chicago fire was in 1871.
○	○	B. The fire burned for nearly thirty hours.
○	○	C. Over seventeen thousand buildings were destroyed.
○	○	D. The reporter didn't know the fire's cause.

2. You probably know that humans have red blood. So do other mammals. But other kinds of creatures have different colors of blood. Insects have yellow blood, and the blood of the lobster is blue.

Fact	Inference	
○	○	A. Humans have red blood.
○	○	B. Frogs do not have red blood.
○	○	C. Lobsters have blue blood.
○	○	D. Insects have yellow blood.

3. Do you like tomatoes? They taste good on a sandwich or in a salad. But for a long time, people thought tomatoes contained poison. Instead of eating the fruit, people once ate the leaves of the tomato plant. Then they got sick. So they thought the whole plant was bad. For years people would not eat tomatoes because of the fear of poisoning.

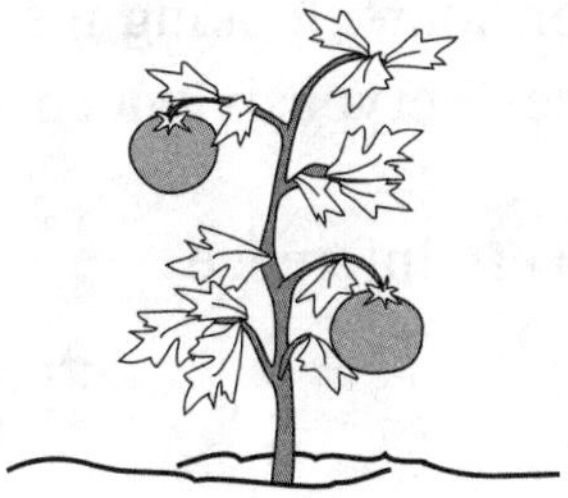

Fact	Inference	
○	○	A. People once thought tomatoes had poison.
○	○	B. Tomato leaves are not good to eat.
○	○	C. For many years people didn't eat tomatoes.
○	○	D. Tomatoes do not have poison.

© Steck-Vaughn Company

Name ____________________ Date ____________

Read the story. Mark whether each statement is an inference or a fact.

1. Dogs are sometimes called "man's best friend," but some dogs are friendlier than others. Some dogs bite many more people than others do. The kind of dog that bites the most is the German police dog. Poodles also often bite people. Sheepdogs, on the other hand, do not bite much at all.

Fact Inference
○ ○ A. German police dogs are not good pets.
○ ○ B. Poodles often bite people.
○ ○ C. Sheepdogs are friendly.
○ ○ D. Dogs are called "man's best friend."

2. A new one-dollar coin was made in 1979. It showed the face of Susan B. Anthony. She was a leader in the fight for women's rights. But the new coin caused many problems. It was about the same size as a quarter. So people often confused the two coins. Many merchants refused to accept the coin. So the dollar coin was not used very often.

Fact Inference
○ ○ A. Susan B. Anthony's face was on a coin.
○ ○ B. The dollar coin was not made after 1979.
○ ○ C. People confused the new coin with a quarter.
○ ○ D. Store owners did not like the new coin.

3. Willy and Louis were starting to get scared. The sun was going down, and the woods around them were growing dark. The two boys were lost! They had been walking for hours, looking for their way out. But they noticed they were only going in circles. Now they nervously watched the shadows grow longer around them.

Fact Inference
○ ○ A. The boys wanted someone to come find them.
○ ○ B. The sun was going down.
○ ○ C. Willy and Louis were lost.
○ ○ D. The boys had not explored the woods before.

© Steck-Vaughn Company

Name ______________________________ Date ______________

Read the story. Mark whether each statement is an inference or a fact.

1. Daniel Boone was an American pioneer. He was born in 1734. As a young man, Boone fought in the French and Indian Wars. Then he decided to move west. He led a group of people to Kentucky. On the way he helped to lay out the Wilderness Road. Later he moved west again. This time he journeyed to Missouri. Boone died there in 1820.

Fact	Inference	
○	○	A. Daniel Boone was born in 1734.
○	○	B. He liked adventure and excitement.
○	○	C. The Wilderness Road goes to Kentucky.
○	○	D. Daniel Boone died in Missouri.

2. The smell of liver made Wally hold his nose. And he thought he would be sick each time he had to taste spinach. Yet there before him sat those two foods, just waiting to be eaten. When his mother left the room, Wally dashed to the window. He scraped his plate clean behind the curtains and hurried back to his seat. When his mother returned, she was surprised at how quickly he had finished his meal. Wally only grinned nervously.

Fact	Inference	
○	○	A. Wally doesn't like liver or spinach.
○	○	B. Wally's mother was surprised he had finished.
○	○	C. Wally scraped his plate behind the curtains.
○	○	D. Wally was supposed to eat liver and spinach.

3. Gwendolyn Brooks is a poet. She was born in Kansas. But she grew up in Chicago. She began to write poems when she was only 13. In 1950 Brooks won the Pulitzer Prize. She won the award for her book of poems called *Annie Allen*. She was the first African-American woman to receive this honor.

Fact	Inference	
○	○	A. Gwendolyn Brooks likes to write poems.
○	○	B. She was born in Kansas.
○	○	C. Brooks won the Pulitzer Prize in 1950.
○	○	D. Her poems are very good.

© Steck-Vaughn Company

Name ______________________ Date ____________

Read the story. Mark whether each statement is an inference or a fact.

1. The English Channel divides England from Europe. One day in 1926, a young woman stood by the channel. She made up her mind to be the first woman to swim across it. Her name was Gertrude Ederle. The swim was hard and rough, but she finished the trip. She swam the 35 miles in less than 15 hours. Her time set a new world record.

Fact	Inference	
○	○	A. A channel divides England from Europe.
○	○	B. Gertrude Ederle liked to swim.
○	○	C. The long swim made Ederle very tired.
○	○	D. Ederle was a fast swimmer.

2. Galveston is a small island off the coast of Texas. In 1900 a great storm destroyed the place. A hurricane blew in from the Gulf of Mexico. A tidal wave covered the island. Thousands of homes were ruined. More than 800 people died. After the storm people returned to the island. Then a seawall was built to hold back the waters of the gulf.

Fact	Inference	
○	○	A. A great storm struck Galveston in 1900.
○	○	B. Not everyone had time to leave the island.
○	○	C. Galveston is on the Texas coast.
○	○	D. A seawall was built after the storm.

3. Arbor Day is now held the last Friday in April. On this day people gather to plant new trees. The first Arbor Day was held in the 1870s in Nebraska. At that time people planted trees for their beauty and shade.

Fact	Inference	
○	○	A. Arbor Day is held in April.
○	○	B. The people in Nebraska liked trees.
○	○	C. Trees give beauty and shade.
○	○	D. The first Arbor Day was in the 1870s.

© Steck-Vaughn Company

COMPREHENSION: GRADE 5
ANSWER KEY

Unit I: Facts

Assessment, pp. 11-12
1. C
2. A
3. B
4. D
5. A
6. C
7. D
8. A
9. C
10. D

Lesson 1, pp. 13-14
1. B
2. A
3. C
4. B
5. C
6. C
7. A
8. B
9. C
10. D

Lesson 2, pp. 15-16
1. D
2. B
3. C
4. A
5. B
6. C
7. A
8. A
9. B
10. D

Lesson 3, pp. 17-18
1. B
2. D
3. A
4. B
5. A
6. C
7. B
8. A
9. D
10. D

Lesson 4, pp. 19-20
1. D
2. C
3. A
4. D
5. D
6. B
7. A
8. A
9. D
10. C

Lesson 5, pp. 21-22
1. C
2. D
3. A
4. B
5. C
6. D
7. A
8. D
9. A
10. B

Lesson 6, pp. 23-24
1. B
2. D
3. C
4. C
5. A
6. B
7. A
8. C
9. A
10. D

Unit II: Sequence

Assessment, pp. 25-26
1. 3, 2, 1
2. A
3. B
4. A
5. B

Lesson 1, pp. 27-28
1. 3, 1, 2
2. B
3. A
4. B
5. C

Lesson 2, pp. 29-30
1. 1, 3, 2
2. B
3. B
4. C
5. B

Lesson 3, pp. 31-32
1. 2, 1, 3
2. B
3. A
4. C
5. A

Lesson 4, pp. 33-34
1. 2, 1, 3
2. C
3. B
4. A
5. A

Lesson 5, pp. 35-36
1. 2, 3, 1
2. B
3. A
4. C
5. A

Lesson 6, pp. 37-38
1. 2, 1, 3
2. C
3. A
4. B
5. A

Unit III: Context

Assessment, pp. 39-40
1. B
2. A
3. C
4. B
5. D
6. C
7. A
8. B
9. D
10. C
11. B
12. A

Lesson 1, p. 41
1. B
2. A
3. A
4. D
5. B
6. C
7. B
8. D

Lesson 2, p. 42
1. D
2. B
3. B
4. A
5. C
6. D
7. A
8. B

Lesson 3, p. 43
1. B
2. A
3. C
4. D
5. C
6. C
7. D
8. B

Lesson 4, p. 44
1. A
2. D
3. C
4. B
5. B
6. A
7. B
8. C

Lesson 5, p. 45
1. A
2. B
3. C
4. B
5. D
6. B
7. C
8. A

Lesson 6, p. 46
1. D
2. B
3. C
4. A
5. A
6. B
7. D
8. C

Lesson 7, p. 47
1. B
2. A
3. B
4. D

Lesson 8, p. 48
1. C
2. B
3. A
4. B

Lesson 9, p. 49
1. C
2. D
3. D
4. A

Lesson 10, p. 50
1. B
2. D
3. A
4. A

Lesson 11, p. 51
1. C
2. D
3. D
4. B

Lesson 12, p. 52
1. C
2. B
3. A
4. B

Unit IV: Main Idea

Assessment, pp. 53-54
1. B
2. C
3. A
4. C
5. A
6. B

Lesson 1, p. 55
1. B
2. B
3. B

Lesson 2, p. 56
1. C
2. B
3. D

Lesson 3, p. 57
1. A
2. B
3. A

Lesson 4, p. 58
1. D
2. C
3. B

Lesson 5, p. 59
1. A
2. D
3. A

Lesson 6, p. 60
1. B
2. B
3. A

Lesson 7, p. 61
1. C
2. A
3. B

Lesson 8, p. 62
1. A
2. B
3. B

Lesson 9, p. 63
1. C
2. B
3. B

Lesson 10, p. 64
1. C
2. A
3. D

Lesson 11, p. 65
1. A
2. B
3. D

Lesson 12, p. 66
1. C
2. A
3. D

Unit V: Conclusion

Assessment, pp. 67-68
1. B
2. C
3. D
4. A
5. B
6. D

Lesson 1, p. 69
1. B
2. C
3. A

Lesson 2, p. 70
1. C
2. D
3. A

Lesson 3, p. 71
1. B
2. A
3. A

Lesson 4, p. 72
1. B
2. A
3. C

Lesson 5, p. 73
1. C
2. C
3. B

Lesson 6, p. 74
1. C
2. B
3. C

Lesson 7, p. 75
1. D
2. D
3. C

Lesson 8, p. 76
1. B
2. D
3. C

Lesson 9, p. 77
1. C
2. B
3. D

Lesson 10, p. 78
1. D
2. A
3. C

Lesson 11, p. 79
1. D
2. C
3. B

Lesson 12, p. 80
1. D
2. B
3. D

Unit VI: Inference

Assessment, pp. 81-82
1. A. F
   B. I
   C. F
   D. F
2. A. I
   B. I
   C. F
   D. F
3. A. I
   B. F
   C. F
   D. I
4. A. F
   B. F
   C. I
   D. I
5. A. I
   B. F
   C. F
   D. F
6. A. I
   B. F
   C. I
   D. F

Lesson,1, p. 83
1. A. I
   B. I
   C. F
   D. F
2. A. F
   B. F
   C. I
   D. I
3. A. I
   B. F
   C. F
   D. I

Lesson 2, p. 84
1. A. I
   B. I
   C. F
   D. I
2. A. F
   B. F
   C. I
   D. F
3. A. F
   B. I
   C. I
   D. I

Lesson 3, p. 85
1. A. I
   B. I
   C. I
   D. I
2. A. I
   B. I
   C. F
   D. F
3. A. F
   B. F
   C. F
   D. I

Lesson 4, p. 86
1. A. I
   B. I
   C. F
   D. I
2. A. I
   B. I
   C. F
   D. I
3. A. I
   B. F
   C. I
   D. I

Lesson 5, p. 87
1. A. F
   B. F
   C. I
   D. F
2. A. I
   B. I
   C. F
   D. F
3. A. I
   B. I
   C. F
   D. F

Lesson 6, p. 88
1. A. F
   B. I
   C. F
   D. I
2. A. I
   B. I
   C. I
   D. F
3. A. F
   B. F
   C. F
   D. I

Lesson 7, p. 89
1. A. I
   B. I
   C. F
   D. F
2. A. I
   B. F
   C. I
   D. I
3. A. F
   B. I
   C. F
   D. I

Lesson 8, p. 90
1. A. F
   B. F
   C. I
   D. I
2. A. F
   B. F
   C. F
   D. I
3. A. I
   B. I
   C. F
   D. F

Lesson 9, p. 91
1. A. F
   B. F
   C. F
   D. I
2. A. F
   B. I
   C. F
   D. F
3. A. F
   B. I
   C. F
   D. I

Lesson 10, p. 92
1. A. I
   B. F
   C. I
   D. F
2. A. F
   B. I
   C. F
   D. I
3. A. I
   B. F
   C. F
   D. I

Lesson 11, p. 93
1. A. F
   B. I
   C. I
   D. F
2. A. I
   B. F
   C. F
   D. I
3. A. I
   B. F
   C. F
   D. I

Lesson 12, p. 94
1. A. F
   B. I
   C. I
   D. I
2. A. F
   B. I
   C. F
   D. F
3. A. F
   B. I
   C. F
   D. F